# The Jesus Sessions

## GETTING BEYOND THE BUMPER-STICKER GOSPEL

John R. Greco

ISBN:  1-4392-5942-9
ISBN-13:  9781439259429

Unless otherwise noted, all Scripture is taken from the HOLY BIBLE, TODAY'S NEW INTERNATIONAL VERSION®. Copyright © 2001, 2005 by Biblica®. Used by permission of Biblica®. All rights reserved worldwide.

"TNIV" and "Today's New International Version" are trademarks registered in the United States Patent and Trademark Office by Biblica®. Use of either trademark requires the permission of Biblica.

Web site addresses listed in this book were current at the time of publication. Please contact the Wild Olive Press via e-mail (publishing@thewildolivepress.com) to report URLs that are no longer operational and replacement URLs if available.

# Table of Contents

# Foreword

*Who are you?* That was the essence of a question posed to a young Jewish rabbi 2,000 years ago by a Roman politician named Pilate. The Jewish rabbi was, of course, Jesus Christ. Pilate, the politician, asked the question to gain a better understanding of the man who had been presented to him by an angry mob looking to have Him executed. While many in first-century Judea had heard of Him, a relatively small number had actually seen Him, and even fewer had heard His teachings or experienced a personal encounter with Jesus. Pilate really didn't have a clue who Jesus was or what He was all about. He had second-hand information and accusations, but no *real* knowledge of Jesus.

Obviously, this wasn't the ideal introduction; it wasn't a "get to know you" soiree at the local country club. However, I think this scene rings true for a lot of people when it comes to what they know of Jesus of Nazareth. Many of us are like Pilate, living our lives in a seemingly normal manner just like anyone else, when suddenly—BOOM!—we are confronted with Jesus. Though we're not standing face-to-face with an Aramaic-speaking Jew who lives down the street and who likes to wear sandals and long hair, we wonder about the historical Jesus and the variety of claims made about Him. The real question we have is just like the one Pilate asked: *Who is Jesus?* You really cannot accept or reject Jesus Christ without first finding an answer to that question.

*The Jesus Sessions* will help you answer that question by introducing you to Jesus as He really was (and for those who believe, as He still is). John Greco presents Jesus to us without all of the speculation and hearsay. Using the Scriptures as a faithful guide, John gives us a fresh look at the Son of God, clearing away much of the "Jesus culture" that we so often see in abundance.

I love the way John provides the reader with new and different perspectives on familiar passages. You will enjoy this book as you laugh (a lot, by the way), think, explore, reflect, and reexamine this Jewish Carpenter who claimed to be *God-with-skin-on.* This isn't a history book. It isn't a theology book. It's not a Bible study for the already convinced. It's not an attempt to make Jesus fit into our trendy post-modern prejudices. This isn't the Facebook profile of Jesus. This is a snapshot-guided presentation to catalyze the conversation. So go ahead and ask Jesus, *Who are You?* This question leads to a journey of discovery that may start with the small step of reading *The Jesus Sessions,* but I pray that reading this book will only be the beginning, and that you will get to know Jesus the way John has.

*Kevin Butterfield*
*Lead Pastor, Yarra Valley Vineyard Christian Fellowship*
*Melbourne, Australia*

# From One Sojourner to Another
*Why Another Book About Jesus?*

I've often thought about the number of books produced each year about Jesus, the gospel, and Christian spirituality. It seems like a lot of trees must die needlessly, and everything that could ever be said about the Christian faith has already been said. In fact, there are more books about Jesus than any other person in all of human history. There's just something about His life, His death, and His teachings that has remained inspiring, controversial, intriguing, and life-giving for two thousand years. Books have been written about every aspect of Jesus—from His leadership style to His politics to what kind of car He would drive. So what can *this* book possibly add to the conversation?

To be completely honest, I actually hope there's nothing about Jesus in this book that hasn't been written or said before. My intention has not been to write something new, novel, or trendy about Jesus, but instead to write truth—timeless truth important enough to warrant repetition, rumination, and reflection. In fact, I would say that instead of adding something to the conversation about Jesus, I hope that reading this book will strip away confusion—ideas and impressions that have gotten some of us sidetracked—like you would turn the knob on an old radio to cut out static that's obscuring a good song you want to hear more clearly.

I'm certainly not the world's foremost expert on Jesus or the Gospels. I am merely a lifelong student of the Scriptures (as I believe all of Christ's followers should be). Still, I hope you learn something as you read this book. My desire has been to accurately describe the context, the cultural background, the emotions of the characters, and the central points of each narrative discussed. I have tried to make familiar stories come alive,[1] using perspectives shaped by my own experiences in life. In doing these things, I hope to inspire readers to go back to their Bibles and fall in love with Jesus all over again.

If all this "Jesus stuff" is new to you, I hope this book will serve as a thoughtful introduction to the greatest Liberator-Shepherd-King in history. I know how easy it is for the gospel to get weighed down in antiquated language, the Christian subculture, or generational thinking. For many, Jesus *seems* great (at least, from what they can see of Him), but getting a clear picture of who He really is amidst the political statements, various traditions, and Christian jargon can be quite difficult. I know this problem... I have this T-shirt; I've experienced this difficulty myself, so I'm there with you.

Read this book and you'll read about conversations Jesus had with many different people, but I also hope that the very act of reading these pages will serve as a conversation—one I want to have with you—and I hope the conversation we have while you read will lead to other conversations. At the end of each chapter, I ask some hard questions. While I don't have the answers, I hope they stimulate further conversations with your

---

1  Quotations followed by the biblical reference in parentheses are taken directly from the Bible (*Today's New International Version*). Those without a reference are the author's own paraphrase.

friends, with me (feel free to share with me your comments or thoughts[2]) and hopefully with Jesus Himself.

If I could sit down with you over a cup of coffee and a toasted bagel with cream cheese and tell you about the Jesus I know, I would tell you these stories. So, as you turn the pages, I invite you to read about those sessions wherein Jesus touched the lives of people like you and me. I invite you to discuss these stories with your friends—chew on them, wrestle with them, explore them as if they were some wild, unexplored, and uncharted territory (and for some, they might be). Most of all, however, I hope you'll embrace Jesus' invitation to talk with Him, which might lead to friendship, and then relationship... and then on into the greatest adventure you can possibly imagine.

✵ ✵ ✵

### Why This Book Has a Soundtrack

As you flip through this book, you'll notice that each chapter begins with song suggestions. As you come upon these musical proposals, you might think: *A suggested playlist? What gives? A book with a soundtrack?!*

Wow. You sound a little bothered. You should probably take a moment or two to calm down. Breathe deeply. Count to ten.

Are you ready? Okay. Allow me to explain the song thing. In general, you're right: books don't have soundtracks... except this one does.

You see, I love music, but God blessed me with exactly zero musical ability. Nada. Zilch. I can't sing, I can't dance, I can't play an instrument, I have no rhythm, I can barely clap to a beat, and though I'm not conscious of it when I'm doing it, I often sing louder than is socially acceptable in public. This gap between melodic desire and cruel reality is quite frustrating. I have slowly come to terms with the fact that, as much as I love

---

2   I can be reached via e-mail at john.thejesussessions@gmail.com.

music, it will never be something I can create. Because of this actuality, I must concede my dreams of rock stardom, and admit that I can only be a sharer, rather than a maker, of music.

The songs listed at the beginning of each chapter are songs I would put onto a mix tape to share with you when we meet for coffee (that is, if people still listened to cassette tapes). While these tracks add to the stories being told in this book, they are actually stories unto themselves. For many people, music has the ability to relay truth more powerfully than prose. As I write this, all the songs I've suggested are available on iTunes,[3] so I hope you will download them and support the artists who make the music. And I hope that you enjoy these songs as much as I do.

---

3  If you search iMixes in iTunes for "The Jesus Sessions," you'll find the entire playlist.

# Introduction

This book is about the *gospel*—the good news.[4] It's about people who have met Jesus and talked with Him. It's about darkness that was confronted with light and about brokenness that was made whole. The Bible contains four narrative accounts of Jesus' earthly life. We know them as the Gospels—Matthew, Mark, Luke, and John. Included in these narratives are some of the conversations that people had with Jesus. Some of these folks were of little importance in the eyes of the world. Others were wealthy and powerful—the kind of people who appear to lack nothing. Rich or poor, strong or weak, proud or humble, Jesus spoke truth into their lives and pointed the way home.

These stories are in the Bible so that we might see glimpses of ourselves. The Bible says that we are all poor if we are without Christ. And Jesus spent His time on earth preaching good news to the poor—people just like us. These conversations were part of that good news. And, while each

---

4 When Christians use the word *gospel*, which in Greek means simply "good news," we are talking about the common need we all have for a new life. Jesus proclaimed the good news that this new life is available to anyone who comes to Him humbly. The word refers to news so good that because of it, and because of the power it has to change lives, centuries of believers have found true peace and new life. But I'm getting ahead of myself; we'll explore what the gospel is all about over the course of this book...

dialogue is unique, they all bear the unmistakable character of the same Liberator-King, Jesus.

This book is for anyone who's ever had a life-changing conversation with Jesus—*and* for anyone who's ever wanted to. Maybe you haven't spent too much time thinking about Jesus, or maybe you aren't sure what to make of church or Christianity, or maybe you're like me: maybe you grew up in church and you're just tired of religion. For those who have longed to cut through the cultural and social clutter and get at the very heart of God, my hope is that this book will help you see Jesus with fresh eyes.

# CHAPTER ONE
# The Handcrafted, Custom Gospel
The Reason Jesus Came

✡ ✡ ✡

## Luke 4:16-30
## Jesus' Mission Statement

✡ ✡ ✡

**SUGGESTED LISTENING**

Sara Groves: "Conversations," from *Conversations*

Waterdeep: "My God Has Come to Save Me," from *You Are So Good To Me*

# The Handcrafted, Custom Gospel
## The Reason Jesus Came

We were traveling across the United States for the second time in six months. My wife Melinda was driving our Volkswagen while I followed in a rented moving truck. Normally, driving in separate cars would make a trip like this painfully boring, but traveling this way gave me the opportunity to fulfill a childhood fantasy. As a kid, one of my favorite movies was *Smokey and the Bandit*. If you've never seen the film, let me explain why it was such a favorite. About 85 percent of the movie is car chases, and as a seven-year old, I could think of nothing that could have improved the movie (except for maybe adding a car chase or two). We didn't have CB radios and our VW was not exactly a black '77 Trans-Am with a flaming eagle on the hood, but we *did* have walkie-talkies and a long way to travel, so we took advantage of the opportunity to use trucker handles and CB lingo as we drove.

I grew up in New England and, while I'd spent time on both coasts, up until that year I hadn't explored too much of the geography between the two shorelines. When we had driven out to California on our first trip, just a few months earlier, venturing down I-40 was a glorious quest, filled with mountains and plains, deserts and farmland, beautiful cities, spectacular vistas, and unexplored Podunk towns—adventure waiting at every rest stop and off-ramp.

This trip, however, was different. We had already been down this road, albeit in the opposite direction. Without unknown lands and brand-new possibilities ahead of us, the miles ticked by slowly—even with trucker lingo. Still, I was trying to take in as much of the country as I could between sips of horrible gas-station coffee. Who knew when or if I would ever be back this way again?

I think we were making our way eastward across Oklahoma when it came into view—a huge white cross on the side of the road, visible for several miles in either direction because of the flatness of the landscape and the clear weather. In another locale, it would have been an odd sight, certainly a landmark to remember. But these giant crosses seem to be all over the South.

We had passed another such cross just the day before while driving through the Texas panhandle. That one was 190 feet tall and was billed as the second largest cross in the Western Hemisphere. (I didn't realize there was a contest.) I suppose if you're going to commit to building a gigantic symbol for your faith on the side of the highway for everyone to see, you might as well build the biggest; that just goes without saying. I'm sure it was with a measure of shame that they owned up to the designation of "second largest."

As we drew closer to the cross there in Oklahoma, I could see "JESUS SAVES" painted in large red letters on the horizontal bar.

"Breaker… Breaker, do you copy?" came Melinda's voice through my walkie-talkie.

"Roger that. Over," I replied.

"Who is '*Hay-Zoos Sa-vays*'" (pronounced with my wife's best fake Hispanic accent) "and why does he keep writing his name all over the South?" she asked dryly.

"I don't know. The Smokies oughta catch that guy; he's a real public menace. He tagged some church signboards, too. I saw one a couple miles back. Over."

My wife, ever sharp, replies: "Impressive, though… the way he was able to climb up on that big cross and write so legibly."

"True that. Over and out." I smiled and stuck my walkie-talkie back in the other cup-holder—the one that didn't house my cup of gas-station battery acid.

This little exchange got me thinking. I wondered if anyone ever decided to follow Jesus after seeing one of these giant, roadside crosses. I mean, there's not much there. I wondered about what might go through a person's mind after glimpsing one of these monuments. *Jesus saves;* true, *but how? And from what? And what difference should it make to me?* It just didn't seem like drive-by evangelism was the way to go. Think about it; can you picture the scene?

> "Yeah, I had just finished beatin' up some old lady—stole her purse and some jewelry—and I was headed back to pick up my live-in girlfriend at the abortion clinic, but she wasn't out yet, so I decided to rob an orphanage (since I had some time to kill and all). As I peeled out of the parking lot and turned onto Interstate 40, there it

was… a big ol' cross and the words 'JESUS SAVES' in humongous red letters. That was all it took to change my life. Why hadn't anyone told me that before? I pulled off into the break-down lane, knelt down on the side of the road by mile marker forty-two, and surrendered my life to Jesus. In fact, I decided to become a missionary right then and there."

And then our fictional disciple would sigh, lamenting,

"If only I'd seen a bumper sticker with some Christian catch phrase like 'Real Men Love Jesus' or 'My Boss Is a Jewish Carpenter' years earlier, I might not have made so many mistakes with my life."

Now, please don't misunderstand me. I believe with all my heart that Jesus *does* save us. I believe He is the only way to find true contentment and peace in this life and in the life to come. "Believe in Jesus and be saved," says the Bible. It's so simple, but so complex at the same time. What does it really mean to believe in Jesus? [5] When I start thinking about what that phrase means—"to *believe* in Jesus"—the gospel appears

5   Though I hope this will become evident in later chapters, *believing in Jesus* does not refer simply to an intellectual agreement that He was a real person who lived at one time, or that He was a good teacher. When Christians talk of "believing in Jesus," they mean that we are to believe in, trust in, rely upon, depend upon, and utterly obey Him. To be saved—in other words, to be adopted as a child of God, to be rescued from pride, greed, lust, rage, and a myriad of other sins that imprison, and to know that you will spend eternity with Him after you die—one must surrender the control of one's life to Him in complete trust, reliance, dependence, and obedience. If someone tells you that this is easy, don't believe it—and keep a hand on your wallet, too.

to me to be the most beautiful thing in the Universe. And if I begin to ponder the way that such belief impacts my life and the way I see the world, I cannot escape the fact that following Jesus is not simple at all.

Believing the gospel is not a one-time, check-the-box experience; it's never something that should be spoken of solely in the past tense (as in "I walked down the aisle at church when I was seven and accepted Jesus as my Lord and Savior"). The word *believe* is a verb, not a noun that merely describes a state of existence. Salvation is not an airline ticket to heaven—one that you can sit on 'til it's time to fly. A walk with Jesus[6] is something you work at, and (hopefully) enjoy *daily*, like any other relationship you might have with your wife, your parents, your children, or your friends.

In your life, you've probably experienced both good and bad relationships. Bad relationships are those in which communication just doesn't happen, or doesn't happen much. Think of a girl who marries a husband, but then suddenly stops talking to him, ignores his needs, and continues on with her life as though she's not really married at all. She goes out with the girls, flirts with other men, and carries on like she did before she was married. Good relationships, on the other hand, like long and adventurous road trips, are filled with constant communication—unique interactions, deep and rich exchanges, and times of growing closer together—and the result is a thorough alteration of life from the way it had been before the relationship to something that is now altogether new. And, since we are human and don't know the future, good relationships have unexpected turns and unknown landscapes.

---

6  Christians sometimes use the term *walk* to describe a relationship with Jesus. As I kid, when I first started paying attention in church and heard people talk about their "walk with the Lord," I was convinced that Jesus had to be in really good shape with all that walking. I also suspected He must have some holy and righteous reason why He never traveled by car.

Getting to know Jesus is not something that happens in isolation, either. I know it's fashionable to talk about the need for a *personal* Savior (and I do believe nothing could be more personal than when Jesus changes the heart of an individual), but following Jesus is not a solo trek. It's a sojourn made with other pilgrims and refugees. We walk together and talk with each other, sharing our loads, our stories, and our lives, and we learn what God is doing in other people's lives as well. Fellow travelers join us along the way, and our experience is blessed for it, as is our relationship with Jesus.

Our culture has a predisposition toward simplifying everything, including the message of Scripture. We are a people who like sound bites, headline tickers, Cliffs Notes, and Wikipedia. Just give us the gist and we'll be fine. When it comes to the gospel, we utilize everything from colored beads to felt-board reenactments to cheesy pop songs to bumper stickers to well-meaning tracts with numbered steps to signs on the highway which tell us that Jesus saves. We like things that can be compressed, packaged, sanitized, filtered, mass-produced, and made family-friendly. We want once size to fit all. We don't want to think about anything too much, especially something we might have to wrestle with. We don't want truth that might hit us right in the gut, that might require us to change, or that might necessitate our giving things up—things we think we need (or things we just want). We want something straightforward and easy, reducible to the simplest of formulas, and something that doesn't put any unexpected burdens on us. But what if following Jesus can't be done using a formula? What if, instead of being like some algorithm you learned in algebra class—an equation with repeatable steps—a relationship with Jesus is more like geometry?

Geometry deals with size and shape, volume and depth, distance and perspective. Maybe a relationship with Jesus has more in common with those things than with simple, linear formulas. Here's what I mean: Think about a diamond. Think about a three-dimensional, multi-faceted shape big enough to fill a room. Now, imagine this room has many doors—entrances to the room from a multitude of directions. Anyone seeing the shape through one of these doorways would immediately identify it as a diamond, yet its appearance would be unique to each. Their impression would be largely framed by the particular door through which they entered—that unique vantage point from which they initially perceived this beautiful diamond.

If that's too abstract, think about baseball. I remember the first time I visited Fenway Park in Boston. I was in college, and a good friend of mine was dating a girl whose father had season tickets to Red Sox home games.[7] One balmy late summer afternoon, he invited me to join him for a game. Our seats were great—the lower tier, right behind home plate. We could see every batter and every pitch. We could hear the umpire as he made the calls, the clap of the ball hitting the catcher's mitt, and the crack of the bat whenever there was a base hit. We could feel the energy of the baseball game—the excitement of being a part of an American tradition.

Though I'd been to major league ballparks before, I'd never experienced a game like this, and I'd never enjoyed such great seats. Growing up, we usually sat in the bleachers at baseball games, so high up and so far away that we could barely see what was happening. Other times, our seats were

---

[7] I don't recommend dating a girl just because her father has Red Sox tickets, but hey, my friend did eventually marry the young lady, so who am I to say?

close to the field, but they were behind the left field wall; we needed a pair of binoculars to see who was batting. As any baseball fan will tell you, where you sit in relation to the baseball diamond greatly affects how you see and enjoy the game. It changes the experience altogether.

In the same way, experiencing Jesus is a lot like a baseball game. Your perspective will change depending upon your seat—that spot where He comes into view. If you come to Him from one particular place—from some specific or unique point of need—the good news about Jesus will seem to be one thing, comprised of specific content, and it may pack a particular wallop for you. When someone else, sitting in a different part of the ballpark of life—with their own needs, struggles, and life experiences—encounters Him, they'll perceive Him another way, and He may meet their very different need in a very different way. Maybe this is why a relationship with Jesus and the message of the gospel—that written or spoken word that describes that relationship—is sometimes difficult to explain; and maybe too that is why it's often not easily accepted. If having a relationship with Jesus was simply a matter of following a formula, anyone could walk through the steps; the gospel could be presented the same way every time, like a pre-recorded message about a product you simply must have.

Think about a kid with his Red Sox hat skewed sideways, his trusty glove in his hand, and a pocket full of baseball cards. Picture him leaving Fenway after having watched the game from behind the left field wall. As he walks into the parking lot, he might overhear some other folks (who had better seats) talking about the game—how exciting it was, and how there's nothing quite like being at the ballpark. But hold on a second; this description doesn't match his experience. He was there too, but he would freely admit there were times when he couldn't quite see what was going on. He might even have spent the majority of the game staring at the Jumbotron above center field, so his view of the game was no more dynamic than it would have been had he stayed home and watched it on television. The confusion this little kid experiences as he listens to those other spectators in the parking lot after the game is the same puzzlement Christians sometimes cause when they present a one-size-fits-all, prepackaged gospel—when we push out a single, homogenized version of how to enter into a relationship with Jesus. Such a version might truly speak to the hearts of some, but for many it's just not going to match their real-life experiences. It won't reach them; it won't touch them. To some, the phrase "Jesus saves" is utterly meaningless.

Before we continue, I want to make one thing clear: What I am *not* suggesting is that there is more than one gospel or that there is more than one way to God. Jesus is the only way we can be saved. He said, "I am the way and the truth and the life. No one comes to the Father except through me" (John 14:6).[8] Jesus had no competition in this regard. Only by coming to Jesus in humble faith, by following his teachings, and by permitting Him unfettered sovereignty over our lives, can any of us be made righteous before God, receive forgiveness for our sins, and enter into the kingdom of heaven.[9]

As I read through the Gospels, I am struck by the fact that Jesus Himself didn't use formulas. He didn't oversimplify things and He didn't hand out tracts. Instead, He talked with people, and as He did, He tailored each conversation to meet

---

8  Throughout this book, you'll see Scripture references that look like "John 14:6," or "Luke 4:16-30." Sometimes Christians think that everyone knows how to interpret this shorthand. What "John:14:6" means is that you can find the reference in the Gospel of John, in the fourteenth chapter, in verse 6. "Luke 4:16-30" refers to verses sixteen through thirty of the fourth chapter of the Gospel of Luke. And so on...

9  More on this *kingdom* business in Chapter Eight.

that individual at their greatest point of need.[10] With one, He discussed living water; with another, the need to be born again. He asked some to give up everything they had. From others, He asked only for a bite to eat. Sometimes He declared God's favor. At other times, He used harsh and terrifying words. Jesus didn't proclaim a pre-packaged McGospel from the value menu that could be reproduced in every culture and speak to every person's heart in exactly the same way.

✳ ✳ ✳

**Jesus' Mission Statement**

At the beginning of his ministry, Jesus announced to the world His mission statement. In the synagogue of His hometown of Nazareth, He stood up and read a small portion from the book of Isaiah:

> *"The Spirit of the Lord is on me, because he has anointed me to proclaim good news to the poor. He has sent me to proclaim freedom for the prisoners and recovery of sight for the blind, to set the oppressed free, to proclaim the year of the Lord's favor."*
> —*Luke 4:18-19; cf. Isaiah 61:1-2; 58:6*

When he finished reading, He made this remarkable statement: "Today this scripture is fulfilled in your hearing" (Luke 4:21). With these words, Jesus proclaimed that *He* was the embodiment of Isaiah's prophecy, and He declared to the world in no uncertain terms precisely why He had come. He was to

---

10 We shouldn't forget, though, that Jesus very often presumed that the people He was talking with had read, or should have read, the Old Testament Scriptures. Many times in His talks with people He referred to God's written Word, and considered it a given that they would view that Word as a source of inviolable authority. That's why we who live twenty centuries later and who may not have grown up studying the Bible sometimes miss what's going on in these conversations.

be Liberator and Savior—but to each person that would mean something different. For the prisoner, He would grant a pardon. For those living in darkness, He would be a great light. For the oppressed, He would secure release. And for those in debt, He would bring a Year of Jubilee when all the balance sheets would be wiped clean.

The words of Jesus, as recorded in the Bible, were not given in a vacuum. There is no list of commandments and proverbs given without a context; no statement of faith or dogma to be memorized. What we have in the four Gospels is the story of Jesus' life, death, and resurrection. But within that story, we have the remarkable words of the Messiah. At times, Jesus spoke to thousands at once, creating a spontaneous, open-air, megachurch service. At others, He spoke to His band of disciples privately, giving them something not meant for the larger crowds. The Gospel writers also recorded several occasions when Jesus spoke one-on-one with someone in need. These conversations were unique and personal; they were sometimes scandalous and sometimes heartbreaking, but they always changed lives. What else would we expect from private encounters with the great Redeemer of history?

*God loves individuals.* For many, this may be an incredibly radical idea. If you randomly polled people on the street, I'm sure most would tell you that God loves the world. Hey, that's even in our favorite Bible verse, right? "For God so loved the world…" (John 3:16). God loves everyone; that's a no-brainer, and everyone has seen at least one football game on television where this message has been proclaimed to the world during every field goal and extra-point attempt. But to say that God loves *you*, the person reading this book right now (yes, *you!*) is quite another thing. Without even realizing it, we can dismiss that notion out of hand, or at the very least, minimize its power tremendously. We think it a matter of course that God loves everyone, and since I'm a part of that *everyone*, then I guess by default He must love me. *So what?* we say to ourselves. *What's the big deal? If everyone is special, no one is special. If God loves everyone the same, then I'm nobody special to Him.*

But that's *not* who God is and that's *not* the way He loves us. If you have children, ask yourself: Do you love them all? Sure you do. Is each special? Each one definitely is. Does that mean that none of them are special? Not on your life.

In the beginning, when God created Adam, the Bible says God formed him "from the dust of the ground" (Genesis 2:7). He could have spoken man into being as He had done with most of the Universe, but instead, God got His hands dirty. We see from this that even from the start of human history, from His very first interaction with mankind, God has wanted to be intimately involved with us.

In Jesus, God got His hands dirty once again, putting on flesh and coming into the world in the humblest of circumstances. The King of kings was not born in a palace, separated from common humanity. He was born in a stable, in a backwater town, the child of a humble teenage girl who was found to be pregnant before she was married. Jesus was placed in a feeding trough shortly after His birth. The braying and neighing, the grunts and barks, and the chirps and cheeps of farm animals filled His hears; the smells of a stall filled His nostrils.

As an adult, Jesus wasn't above touching the sick or the lame—those considered "unclean" by the Jewish people. He didn't shy away from defending the poor or the oppressed, and He frequently ignored the social mores of the time, chatting with Samaritan women and eating with tax collectors and other notorious sinners. He never, *ever* shrank with fear when He faced the religious leaders of the time—and keep in mind that these leaders had the power to put people out of the synagogue, the local center of Jewish life and faith. They had the ability to remove a person from their village, ruin them socially and economically, and make them a stranger to their own family. Yet Jesus regularly confronted these leaders in order to teach the people an important lesson, or to heal someone who was suffering under the weight of disease or oppression. He even made time for children. Jesus' ministry was messy and controversial. It was sometimes confrontational, sometimes scandalous, but no matter the situation, He faithfully revealed the very heart of God—a heart that longs to welcome each lost child home.

Paying special attention to the interactions Jesus had with individuals then can be incredibly helpful today. These conversations show us how Jesus related to people just like us; how He saw through the outer appearance and spoke to the person's unique situation. Without preconditions, Jesus talked with people right where they were. In that intensely religious, traditional Jewish culture, with all its laws and proscriptions and penalties, certain people were to be avoided. But for Jesus, there was no sin too black, no shame too grievous, to keep Him from sharing the message of hope with someone in need.

But here is the incredible thing: *This hasn't changed in two thousand years.* God *still* wants to talk individually with those who desire to know Him. He knows your greatest struggles and He knows mine. He knows our greatest weaknesses; He knows our worst sins... and *still* He longs to speak words of reconciliation into our lives. These words are the very heart of the gospel itself.

Jesus did not come with bumper stickers or sound bites or with His message scrawled across a giant ornamental cross on the highway. The people He came to save could not be helped with fast-food religion. God made each of us a unique and special creation, and as such we each have our own issues and baggage, our own future to walk through, and our own responses to this fallen world. *That* is where Jesus wants to meet us—at the deepest point of our greatest need.

✵ ✵ ✵

*"I have come that they may have life, and have it to the full."*
*(John 10:10b)*

Chapter One: The Handcrafted, Custom Gospel
Questions for Reflection & Discussion:

1) Whether or not you would identify yourself as a Christian, how would you explain the gospel message to someone else?

2) What do you think about the author's statement, "Jesus didn't proclaim a pre-packaged McGospel from the value menu that could be reproduced in every culture and speak to every person's heart in exactly the same way"? Is there a danger in this line of thinking?

3) Have you ever had difficulty believing God loves you? If so, why do you think that is?

CHAPTER TWO

# Green Eggs and Mammon

The One Thing that Matters

☆ ☆ ☆

## Luke 18:18-30
## The Rich Young Ruler

☆ ☆ ☆

**SUGGESTED LISTENING**

Derek Webb: "Rich Young Ruler," from *Mockingbird*

Poor Rich Folk: "The Suffering Wealthy," from *The Suffering Wealthy* (Digital Single)

# Green Eggs and Mammon
## The One Thing that Matters

There was once a young man who possessed wealth and power and all the respect those things could buy. Yet, somehow he knew something was missing.

One day, he met another man, a man who did not have wealth or power, at least not in the way the young man measured those things. Still, the rich young power broker knew that this itinerant preacher had something special. And, as he did whenever he wanted something, he approached the Galilean with an energetic smile and a spring in his step—after all, you only get one chance to make a first impression. As he got closer, though, he realized that it might be more appropriate to bow down in reverence. He'd heard the rumors and debates about this preacher; He might very well be a prophet sent from God. So, stooping low, the young man humbled himself.

When he stood, he got right to the heart of the matter: "Good teacher, what must I do to inherit eternal life?" (Luke 18:18).

Until recently, the story of the rich young ruler was lost on me. I grew up attending church, so I'd heard the account hundreds of times. Familiarity with the Bible can be a wonderful thing, but without an equally intense passion for the heart of God, it can also dull us to the power of the Bible's message... and that can be more dangerous than never having heard truth at all. If we're not careful, we can become like some of the Pharisees and teachers of the law Jesus encountered. They certainly knew the Hebrew Scriptures, but many of them missed the very heart of God.

A few months ago, I tried reading the story of the rich young ruler as if it were brand-new, as if I'd never read it before. I stopped after each sentence and thought deeply about the words. I tried to put myself into the story. I thought about how I would have reacted if I were the rich young ruler. I also thought about what would have happened if, instead of the real Jesus, the ruler had encountered the Jesus often found in many corners of the Evangelical Christian subculture—a Jesus who slavishly follows a mapped-out gospel presentation, and who's more concerned with getting a seeker to say the Sinner's Prayer than he is with the individual's heart. Sadly, it may be that this modern American Jesus is more familiar to many of us than the Jesus revealed in Scripture (and we might be more comfortable with our version too).

Putting myself in this false Jesus' place, my gut reaction would've been to tell the rich young man that I didn't care about his money or his power; he needed to "accept me into his heart." I would then have asked him to bow his head and repeat the Sinner's Prayer after me—only it would be much more specific than the generic prayer, because as Jesus I would know everything the young man had ever done and be able to nail down every specific sin the young ruler would need to confess. Should he stumble up against some early doubts, such a display of omniscience would surely impress the young ruler and confirm his decision to accept me into his heart.

Once we finished praying, I would tell him to read his Bible every day, starting with the book of John (though he would have to wait a few decades for John to write it). I'd also tell him to get plugged in to a local church and find a good small group, maybe one studying *The Purpose-Driven Life* or *The Prayer of Jabez*.

There is certainly a time and place to apply particular strategies when evangelizing, but if you've read the story of the rich young ruler before, you know that Jesus didn't give him a three-point gospel presentation, nor did He lead him in the Sinner's Prayer. Instead, Jesus began by running through the Ten Commandments. This must have set the young man's heart at ease, because without flinching and with a straight face, he was able to say, "All these I have kept since I was a boy" (Luke 18:21). Amazingly, Jesus didn't argue with him.

Again, if I were the simple Jesus of pop-Christianity, I would have done things differently after hearing the young man's brazen assertion that he'd kept all the commandments. I would have pulled out a rolling cart with a TV/DVD combo from behind a grove of palm trees and played clips from the man's life, showing (in graphic detail) all his moral failures. It would have been convicting and humbling at the same time, and it would have taught him not to bluff the Son of God. But Jesus didn't do that. According to one version of the story, we're told that Jesus looked at the wealthy young man *and loved him* (see Mark 10:21). What did the real Jesus do then? He told the young man to sell all his possessions and give the money to the poor.

I'm sure the ruler was shocked at Jesus' instructions. After all, in that culture, in that time, money was supposed to be a sign of God's blessing and approval.[11] The rich young ruler isn't the only one who should be shocked by Jesus' response. I've never heard a television preacher end a sermon with a plea for viewers at home to liquidate their assets and give to the homeless in their area.[12]

Maybe you're like me and you've heard the story so many times that your ears have become deaf to its power. Or maybe this is the first time you've ever heard it. Either way, it's easy to fill our minds with rationalizations that would explain the command given by Jesus for the young man to empty his bank accounts, isn't it? We say to ourselves, *Surely the young ruler deserved it; he probably didn't appreciate God's blessings… or maybe Jesus knew that he beat his wife or earned his money doing something unethical, like selling poor-quality olive oil on the black market, or dealing drugs to small children.* But no, the Bible tells us that Jesus' instruction wasn't a punishment. The text tells us specifically that it was because Jesus loved the wealthy young man that He issued this command.

The Bible also tells us that the rich young ruler left feeling dejected. Thinking with my typical American church mind, I can imagine one of the disciples chasing after him.[13] He would apologize profusely for Jesus' behavior back there, all the time thinking, *What was Jesus doing? We don't want to offend our wealthy patrons. If the Son of God had played His cards right, at least for a few minutes, He could've secured our ministry's solvency for years to come!*

---

11 Sometimes it feels like the cultural differences between first-century Israel and twenty-first century America are razor thin.

12 The subject of giving money away *does* come up during these shows, but somehow it always works out that the evangelist himself is the one most in need of our contributions.

13 It probably would have been Peter. Reading through the Gospels, it's clear that Peter had a good heart but an impulsive nature.

So what about this young man? Why did he have to do something so drastic to be saved? Why didn't Jesus tell him that we're not saved by our works? After all, it's all about grace, right? Why did Jesus seemingly change the rules for this one guy?

To be honest, when I first began to contemplate the story of the rich young ruler, I was somewhat worried. Jesus didn't trip over His words; there could be no misunderstanding about what He expected the powerful young man to do. And then I thought, *What if there's something Jesus expects* me *to do? What if it's something that would make me cringe or that would make it not so easy to follow Him?*

For the young ruler, there was no way around it. He couldn't just pretend to sell everything he had; Jesus would know. And he couldn't very easily reinterpret what Jesus had said in some other, less radical way. I can just hear him telling his friends, "Meeting with Jesus was great. He's a real straight-shooter; you'd like Him. He told me how much He admired my success, but suggested that I rearrange my portfolio in order to invest in some socially-conscious mutual funds. I'm going to consider it. After all, it's always good to help those less fortunate, and everyone's got to do their part." Then he would closet himself privately for a few minutes and weep, knowing he had chosen money over his very soul.

Jesus spoke about money quite often, but not in the sleazy way some preachers on TV are prone to do. Jesus talked about the spiritual dangers that can come from having too much of it, and how true security comes only from God. He also talked about the importance of helping others, especially those in need. He even made this bold statement: "You cannot serve both God and Money" (Luke 16:13). I'm pretty sure Jesus meant this statement as a matter of fact, but some people seem to live their lives as if He meant it as a challenge, holding tightly to both their wallets and their Bibles.

No, there is no getting around Jesus' words. Maybe that's why we read over the story of the rich young ruler so quickly and why we are glad for the story's familiarity. If the full power of His words really struck us, we might have to think hard about what drastic, life-changing thing Jesus might ask of us... and that's a scary thought. It's a thought that doesn't easily fit into our notions of following Jesus. We're taught to be seeker-sensitive—to never turn a seeker away—so it's hard to imagine Jesus doing that very thing. Yet, we can't gloss over the fact that the young seeker went away downcast and without the assurance of eternal life he had so enthusiastically sought.

✲ ✲ ✲

I have a part-time job teaching a high school Bible course. Even though it's a Christian high school, most of the students in my class have had little or no exposure to Scripture. As such, they ask a lot of questions, which is great. It makes class a lot more fun. However, the most common questions I get have to do with boundaries. They want to know where the line is; they want to know what they can get away with without making God angry.

"Mr. Greco, what if someone does something *really* mean to you? Then is it okay to get back at them?"

"What if I'm at a party and I have a drink, but it's only beer, and what if I don't get drunk, and I don't drive? It's not that bad a sin then, right?"

"He's not a Christian, but he's a really nice guy. I think if I witness to him while I'm dating him, he might be ready to accept Jesus. Is it okay to go out with him?"

My students are keenly aware that sin is enjoyable. At first, I thought that this inclination to flirt so closely around the edges of sin might be due to their youth. I reasoned that more mature people would recognize that sin is something to be avoided. But the more I pondered my students' questions, the more I realized that age and physical maturity have nothing to do with one's attitude toward sin. I think we all—regardless of our age—like to sin, at least on a certain level. After all, guilty pleasures wouldn't be a temptation if they weren't pleasurable. To their credit, these students were just asking honest questions; they were not hiding behind a wall of artificial piety (which one *does* sometimes see with "age and maturity").

However, the truth remains: Sin is really something to be sacrificed if they are going to follow Christ. I always emphasize that the Christian life is not merely a list of *do*s and *don't*s, but an overflowing life lived in relationship with Jesus.

Some explanation may be needed here; I can imagine that someone unfamiliar with some of the Christian jargon I've just tossed out might wonder what an *overflowing life* looks like. An overflowing life is a life in which the Spirit of Jesus informs and governs the choices we make. It's a life in which, instead of wandering around aimlessly, or worse—following our own selfish desires to what we think will bring us true happiness—the One who created us leads us to find our true purpose, and our true joy. After all, no one knows how we're wired better than the One who wired us. Though it's common to think of the restrictions that come with following Jesus, that image alone is not really an accurate picture. What we gain from obedience—true freedom to live and walk as we were meant to be, in step with the Spirit—is so much more than what we give up.[14] And it really is an overflowing life!

Jesus loves us despite our poor judgment, our selfishness, our idolatry, and our addictions. Salvation is not something we earn; Jesus already did everything necessary on our behalf. In some ways, though, I think the line of questioning in my classroom is wise. It's important to know what you're signing up for. Even Jesus told people they should think long and hard before making up their minds about Him—before signing up for a life of obedience under His sovereignty. After all, you can't follow Jesus by heading in the opposite direction.

On one occasion, He put it this way: "Suppose one of you wants to build a tower. Won't you first sit down and estimate the cost to see if you have enough money to complete it? For if you lay the foundation and are not able to finish it, everyone who sees it will ridicule you, saying, 'This person began to build and wasn't able to finish'" (Luke 14:28-30).

But there we go again with this business about *cost*. Salvation is supposed to be free, isn't it? It's supposed to be about grace. Doesn't Jesus read His own press? Why would He ask us to give up something in return for salvation?

In the book of Proverbs, there is a prayer that is both beautiful and shocking to modern ears. It's the kind of prayer I think could radically change a church community if it were on the lips of God's people:

---

14 A note about obedience may be necessary here. Though the word can conjure images of house-training a puppy or of slave labor, that's not at all what obeying Jesus looks like. It's better to think of it in terms of a parent's love. A good parent wants their children to be obedient because they love their kids and want what's best for them. It's out of that obedience that the child matures, develops character, and learns to function in society. A very good parent can even identify areas in which their children thrive and can guide them to make choices that will benefit them later in life. God's knowledge of what is good for us is infinitely better than our earthly parents' understanding, so His ways really are best.

*"Two things I ask of you, LORD; do not refuse me before I die: Keep falsehood and lies far from me; give me neither poverty nor riches, but give me only my daily bread. Otherwise, I may have too much and disown you and say, 'Who is the LORD?' Or I may become poor and steal, and so dishonor the name of my God."*
—*Proverbs 30:7-9*

Agur, the man to whom this prayer is attributed, hit on something that the apostle Paul will reiterate centuries later: "For the love of money is a root of all kinds of evil. Some people, eager for money, have wandered from the faith and pierced themselves with many griefs" (1 Timothy 6:10). It's easy to ask God to spare us from a life of poverty, but it's not as easy to ask Him to spare us from a life of wealth, yet both can be a problem if we let a preoccupation with money stand between us and God.

In America, we don't like to give things up. We are a nation of individuals who want just one more thing, who are loath to let anything go; we want it *all*. We want a large house and two luxury cars in the driveway, but we *also* want jobs that will allow us plenty of quality time with the family. We want our careers to fulfill us *and* fill our wallets. We want meaningful relationships *and* plenty of time to ourselves. We want to be healthy, attractive, and sexy, *and* don't want to worry about what we eat, nor do we want to exercise. We want our government to take care of us, *and* we don't want our taxes to increase. In a phrase, *we want it all*.

We are a lot like Abbie, the Golden Retriever I had growing up. She was fetch-challenged, unwilling to return with a ball that had been tossed to her. No matter how much you called her name, clapped your hands, or whistled, she would ignore you once she had that tennis ball in her jowls. Abbie wasn't a bad dog, and it wasn't that she didn't like the attention; she just really enjoyed tearing a tennis ball to shreds. So, to have a real game of fetch with her, I needed to have two tennis balls at the ready. After I threw one, she would race out into the yard and recover it; she would lose no time destroying it. The only way to get her attention then was to throw the other ball in the opposite direction. The enticement of the new ball was enough to get her to drop the first and head off running after the second. Then I could pick up the first (now soggy) ball just in time to draw her away from the newly retrieved second ball. And so on and so on…

The thing Abbie *really* wanted to do—to destroy a tennis ball—was always just out of reach, because there was always another ball yanking at her attention, luring her away. I think money, or anything else that we value more than God, is to us what that second tennis ball was to Abbie.

Jesus doesn't ask us to give things up to be mean or because He wants us to be unhappy. In fact, I think it's just the opposite. He knows that nothing other than Him will ever make us truly happy or truly free, but as long as there's something else our heart wants more than Him, we'll never be able to fully embrace Him; we'll never be able to understand and receive and grow with Him.

I think it's different for everybody. For some, their struggle is like the rich young ruler's—money is in the way. For others, it's power, position, or comfort that's the problem. Some tennis balls are easy to spot; some are hidden in the tall grass of life, so to speak. Some would even be considered good things, if they weren't standing in the way of something better. Regardless, we all need to identify those things that block us from truly following Jesus.

C. S. Lewis wrote about this very problem in *The Weight of Glory and Other Addresses*: "We are half-hearted creatures, fooling about with drink and sex and ambition when infinite joy is offered us, like an ignorant child who wants to go on making mud pies in a slum because he cannot imagine what is meant by the offer of a holiday at the sea. We are far too easily pleased." Jesus wants us to put aside the inferior things—those things that seem to promise us contentment, but instead deliver only temporary, plastic pleasure—in order to obtain something far better.

When I think about my own life, I am struck by how many times I've chosen slum-made mud-pies instead of the beach. If I put myself into the story of the rich young ruler, it probably wouldn't be money Jesus would ask me to give up (I don't have much). But, over the years, there have been numerous things I've allowed to get between Him and me. Relationships, status, possessions, pride, and my own comfort are the least embarrassing ones to admit here, but none are worth the price.

Abundant, eternal life is free, but it costs us everything. For those who can't let go of whatever it is they value more than Jesus, the price seems just too steep. But when we actually put Him first, by our actions and with our will, that thing—whatever it was we thought was so priceless—is revealed in clear light to be worthless. In hindsight, it was not something to be sacrificed at all, but rather something like a ball and chain; something from which we eventually rejoice to be set free. No sane man laments the loss of his chains once he is released.

The New Testament doesn't tell us if the young ruler ever came to his senses and sold his possessions in order to follow Jesus, but I'd like to think he did. I'd like to think that as he was giving his once-precious money to the poor, they asked him why he was being so generous. Such charity would not only have freed the young man's soul, but it also would have been a catalyst to help others see Jesus. His actions would show a truer picture of Jesus than any sermon ever could. And I'd like to think that as the young man emptied his pockets and saw Jesus changing lives all around him, he found that he'd become richer than ever before.

✠ ✠ ✠

*"'Truly I tell you,' Jesus said to them, 'no one who has left home or wife or brothers or sisters or parents or children for the sake of the kingdom of God will fail to receive many times as much in this age, and in the age to come eternal life.'" (Luke 18:29-30)*

**Chapter Two: Green Eggs and Mammon**
**Questions for Reflection & Discussion:**

1) Put yourself in the place of the rich young ruler. If Jesus asked you to give up all your possessions in order to follow Him, would you do it?

2) Do you think the author's portrayal of "the Jesus of pop-Christianity" is fair? Why or why not?

3) Take a few minutes to think and pray about your own life. Is there something standing between you and God—something you believe He might be asking you to give up?

# All Shall Be Well
## Leaving the Past Behind

✫ ✫ ✫

---

# John 4:1-42
# The Woman at the Well

---

✫ ✫ ✫

## SUGGESTED LISTENING

Jennifer Knapp: "Lay It Down," from *Lay It Down*

Sandra McCracken: "And Can It Be," from *Indelible Grace*

# All Shall Be Well
## Leaving the Past Behind

If you've ever seen the film *The Ring*, you know that the title refers to the final perspective of a little girl being sealed inside a deep, old, country well. She looks up as daylight is eclipsed by a large stone slab. A ring of sunlight is visible around the edges until the final moment when that well becomes a grave. The image on screen is decidedly unsettling.

Though the entire movie is supposed to be scary, in my opinion, the view from the bottom of the well is the most eerily haunting image in the film. I can imagine no lonelier place. Think of it—being sealed inside a small, dark, cold, watery hole, deep beneath the earth. It would be pitch-black. No one could hear you cry out. Any sound you heard would either be unwelcome vermin intrigued by the well's new occupant or the first indication that your mind is coming unhinged. It's probably one of the best depictions of hell I've ever seen.

Like a small child who's become lost in a crowd and who's just realized that his parents are nowhere in sight, panic sets in when we think we've been abandoned... that is, unless there's a particularly good reason why being alone has become attractive.

The Bible tells us a story about another well. But this well was not normally a lonely place. It was instead a place for conversation, for laughter, and a place where gossip was exchanged with a sense of urgency that far surpassed the need for water. It was a place where, daily (and sometimes twice daily), women from the Samaritan village of Sychar would gather to collect water for their households. Not only would they collect water, they would also collect stories and assorted gossip. These housewives would catch up with each other's lives while sharing the latest news and scandals of the village. They would come first thing in the morning, before the heat of the day struck with its full force. Gathering and carrying water was hard work and doing so under the broiling Middle Eastern sun was to be avoided if at all possible.

So this well was not normally a lonely place. But for one woman in the village, it was exactly that—and she preferred it that way. She purposely chose the hottest time of the day to fetch her water. For her, it was worth enduring the scorching sun, if only to avoid the stares, the snickers, and the humiliation that would surely come if she went to the well when it was cooler, when other (more respectable) women were there.

There was one day, though, when she was not alone despite her planning. As she approached the familiar watering hole, she spied a silhouette; it was a man. As she came closer, she could see it was a Jewish man. *No problem here*, she thought. *He's obviously a stranger; he doesn't belong to this village, so he doesn't know me or what I've done. And besides, he's Jewish. He'll probably leave as he sees me approaching. He surely doesn't want my "filth" to rub off on him.* She reached the well, but He didn't move away. And then, to the woman's shock, the man spoke to her: "Will you give me a drink?" (John 4:7).

This Jewish man was, of course, Jesus. And with those few words, He broke through a crusted wall built from generations of racism, prejudice, and injustice.

Jews did not normally interact with Samaritans. Jews viewed them as "unclean" because they were of a mixed race, the descendents of Jews from northern Israel and Assyrians who had invaded the country centuries earlier. They had their own version of the Bible and had even built their own local temple. As a result, there was a lot of tension between Jews and Samaritans. Most Jews would avoid the whole region of Samaria altogether, and they certainly wouldn't think of asking a Samaritan for a drink of water. So, Jesus' simple request was out of the ordinary, to say the least. It was the equivalent of a white man asking a black man to join him at the front of the bus in the segregated South of 1935.

And beyond the issue of race, a Jewish man in Jesus' day would not normally converse with any woman who was not his wife or close relative. If there were any onlookers, this scene would have been scandalous indeed.

The Samaritan woman had been trying to steer clear of people. Ironically, she kept her shameful past covered in darkness only by visiting the well when the light of the sun was most intense. Jesus, however, knew everything she had ever done. She could not hide from His light, no matter how hard she tried.

At first, she simply pointed out the absurdity of the request: "You are a Jew and I am a Samaritan woman. How can you ask me for a drink?" (Luke 4:9). But Jesus turned the tables and spoke to her of *living* water. It was what she needed to once-and-for-all quench her spiritual thirst. Jesus knew that the woman had an insatiable longing to be free from the disgrace and dishonor she had suffered for so many years; her deepest desire was to be securely loved.

With His offer of living water, Jesus was offering her a fresh start—a new life—but she didn't understand. Her mind grabbed on to something He had said: *Never thirst again.* She couldn't shake that thought. *Could it be true? Could there be such water that would forever cure thirst?* That would mean no more trips to this well; no more unkind stares; no more whispers and laughter; no more rejection. She thought about how such water would make it easier to keep her past hidden in darkness… but Jesus was not interested in making her a safe place in the darkness, or in hiding her past. Jesus was (and is still) all about light.

"Go, get your husband. I'll wait," He said. And with that, she got nervous… but only for a second.

"I have no husband to go and get," she replied, thinking that what she was saying was technically true. She was no longer married.

And then everything changed. There would be no more hiding, at least not from Him. Jesus told her, "You are right when you say you have no husband. The fact is, you have had five husbands, and the man you now have is not your husband. What you have just said is quite true" (Luke 4:17-18). Just like the water that she had minutes earlier pulled up from the darkness of the well's depths to the light of the midday sun, Jesus exposed her guilt and shame.

✯ ✯ ✯

On his 2004 live album, *The House Show*, singer/songwriter Derek Webb introduces the song "I Repent" with these words: "The best thing that could ever happen to anybody in this room—the *best* thing—would be that your sin would be literally exposed on the five o'clock news. Your deepest, darkest, most embarrassing sin—the one you work the hardest to hide—would be broadcast on the five o'clock news."[15] Webb's point is that the Christian life is not about hiding from others, especially from other believers. In fact, all the hiding doesn't really protect us at all. It keeps us from the very thing we need most.

Think about that for a moment. Imagine a registry not just for convicted sex offenders, but also for those addicted to Internet porn; a roster of people who hate their neighbors; a manifest with the names of people who steal office supplies; a public list for [name of your sin here]. Imagine the CNN or Fox News headline ticker regularly reporting on your road rage, the lies you put on your résumé, or the fact that you and your girlfriend have been sleeping together. If you're like me, the thought of your sin being broadcast for the entire world to see is a scary thought. Our flesh—that part of each of us that revels in the mire of self—hates it.

Webb goes on to say, "I am so tired of hiding my sin from people, of deceiving people about who I really am. I'm tired of it. I just wish my sins would... be exposed. I wish there were huge screens that would show you the truth about me, all the way down to my core... that I would have nothing but Jesus to grasp onto, because that's all I've got anyway."[16]

Derek Webb is onto something. It's the same thing Jesus was telling the woman at the well: Hiding our sin might alleviate some measure of shame at first, but if hiding in the dark becomes a way of life, it will keep us from what we need most.

---

15 Derek Webb, "Introduction to 'I Repent,'" *The House Show,* © 2004 INO Records LLC.
16 Ibid.

Kids can teach you many things about life. Without even realizing it, they have a lot to say about the human experience. Children do things instinctively that few adults would ever do, even after much consideration. Spend time with a child and you'll see: They are often inappropriately honest.[17] Sometimes their comments are just funny; other times, their innocent clarity of thought reveals overlooked truths about this life. A child's actions can jolt us into seeing things anew, with a fresh perspective, if we take the time to reflect. For example, it has been said that children are born with no prejudices; they have to be taught to hate a person because of their skin color, or because of their religion. Kids don't naturally care about race, creed, or social status. They will make friends with anyone, whether that friendship is based on nothing more than a common love for a favorite cartoon character or the geographic convenience of living next-door to one another. Imagine if instead of sending heads of state or ambassadors to posts in the United Nations, every nation sent their best and brightest six-year olds. I believe extreme poverty would be alleviated and world peace secured before naptime.

My favorite thing about young kids is the way they can find joy in simple things. Until they are shown that "good" toys come in shiny boxes, make lots of noise, and have commercials and cartoons dedicated to them, kids are happy with a discarded refrigerator box (which is in truth a magnificent fort) or with pots and pans from the kitchen (which are really instruments suitable for a grand concert). It doesn't take much. It's as if they know that life should be an adventure and that it's supposed to be fun, so they're always ready.

---

17 I recall my younger brother (at the age of three), pointing out an overweight woman at the grocery store checkout, and to my mother's complete embarrassment, declaring to the world, "She eats!" There was no unkind intention in his saying this; he had just figured out that's how food and weight gain work.

My nephew Mark is a great example. A few years ago, my wife and I stayed with Mark's family for a few months during one of life's many transitions. During that extended stay, Mark taught Melinda and me many things. Mark was about three years old at the time and so he showed us the proper way to walk and roar like a dinosaur. He demonstrated that music is, in fact, not really music if you can't shake your butt to the beat. He also tried to instill in us the idea that the world should stop when *Backyardigans* comes on the TV.

But the best thing Mark taught us came when we played hide-and-seek. Mark loves to play. Regardless of what had his attention (excepting the aforementioned *Backyardigans*), saying "One... two... three..." with just the right inflection in my voice was all it would take to send him running for a hiding place. I'm pretty sure Mark likes the hiding part better than the seeking, though. Walking into a still, dark room, not knowing if someone is hiding behind the door can be quite scary for a three-year old. But, when it's his turn to hide, he lights up.

I make my way slowly around the corner, announcing, "Ready or not, here I come!" I hear giggles; I see little, happy feet shuffling from behind the curtains in his parents' bedroom. As I get closer, I tease him: "Where are you Mark?" I say (loudly) to the dog, "Breva, have you seen Mark? I lost him and his mommy and daddy are going to be very upset. Guess I'll have to go back on eBay and order a new nephew..." The giggles from behind the curtain grow louder. Before I can reach him, he jumps into plain view. "Here I am, Uncle John!"

Sadly, Mark will probably never play on a world-champion hide-and-seek team. Still, I think Mark gets something that we often miss. With visible joy in his face, Mark understands that hiding is never the point. It's supposed to end sometime. He wants to be found. His smile reveals the overflowing excitement he has in knowing that someone who loves him is hunting and searching all over the house—in closets, under beds, behind the couch—all just for him. And the best part for Mark? Reappearing to the world and to someone who cares about him.

When we get older, though, we can think of hiding as a way of life. No one needs to see the ugly things in our past; no one needs to really know our heart. And so we put our best face forward. Like a used car salesman trying to unload a freshly painted 1983 Chevy with a worn-out engine and no brakes, we're convinced we can get by in life only showing others what's on the surface. It's not like we plan on keeping our secrets forever or on wearing masks permanently; they just became a part of our routine.

Hiding can be a defense mechanism, a way of keeping pain at a distance. Many people crawl through their lives this way, getting by, continually living in the shadows. But they do only that: *get by.* Jesus offers so much more. With His outstretched arms, He invites us to embrace an abundant, full, meaningful life with Him, lived out in the open. Continuing to hide, living behind walls, just will not do. Simply put, light and darkness cannot occupy the same space, and we must make a choice between them if we are to receive the life Jesus offers.

☆ ☆ ☆

There are a handful of movies that automatically arrest my channel surfing. If they're on, I stop flipping through the channels and watch, no matter how many times I've seen them. One such movie is *The Shawshank Redemption.*

The film is set at a prison in Maine in the 1940s. Andy Dufresne, played by Tim Robbins, is falsely convicted and sent to prison for the murder of his wife. Though Andy's situation appears bleak, he doesn't lose hope. At one point in the film, his friend Red (Morgan Freeman) warns him, "Let me tell you something, my friend. Hope is a dangerous thing. Hope can drive a man insane. It's got no use on the inside. You'd better get used to that idea."

The rest of the movie is a struggle between two ways of life: one lived in hope and the other, in apathy. Andy embodies hope, and it's contagious. Everyone he touches comes back to life, even if just for a little bit.

But the helplessness and fear that come from years in prison are not easily undone. One of the characters in the film, Brooks Hatlen (played by James Whitmore), is an old man who's been at Shawshank for fifty years. Often, Brooks is seen with a crow on his shoulder. The crow's name is Jake, and Brooks has cared for him since he was just a baby bird. To any onlookers, Brooks is kind and gentle, not hardened or angry, the way we often think of long-term prisoners. It seems that if anyone has withstood the crushing fear and depression that come with life behind bars, it is certainly Brooks. In charge of the prison book cart, he has responsibilities and friends. In his own mind, he is an important person in the world.

Late in the film, Brooks finds out he is being paroled. He is going to be let out of prison in his old age, but this is not welcome news. To deal with life at Shawshank, he had banished hope from his mind, to the point that the gray walls of his dreary cell now appeared warm and comfortable. Now that freedom is within his grasp, he doesn't want it. At first, he becomes so scared of life on the outside that he flies into a rage, holding a knife to another prisoner's throat in the hope that the authorities would let him stay. After realizing he has no choice but to leave, he calms down. He collects himself and he releases Jake through the bars of a prison window. With a new suit, a job, and a room at a halfway house, he too is released to rejoin the outside world.

Not too long after he leaves prison, he stands on a chair in the bleak boarding house and carves "Brooks was here" into a ceiling beam as a message to any other prisoner who might make their way through that place. It's his last act before hanging himself.

Brooks had gotten so comfortable in prison that his mind could not handle freedom. He simply didn't know what to do with it. Like a drug addict in need of a fix, he had convinced himself that the walls and bars he had known for so long were absolutely necessary. And worse than that, he had become certain that his prison cell was no cage at all, but a safe shelter, protecting him from the dangers of the outside world. We can do the same thing with our past sins and regrets. We can build walls that protect us, but never admit that what we've really built is a prison.

Jesus came to set us free, but we have to first admit to ourselves that we are, in fact, in need of a Liberator. This is an aspect of the gospel we sometimes brush aside. But think of this: If we live our lives as if we have no sins or shortcomings, we must also live as though we have no need of a Savior. Without first acknowledging our need to be set free, we will never come to a place where we can embrace freedom when it is offered. We'll be like Brooks, perfectly content pushing a book cart through our own prison halls, convinced in our own minds that there is no greater freedom to be had. And that is *not* the Christian life.

Freedom comes when we step out of the shame of the past, but we can only do so when we are honest. I'm not suggesting that we begin every new friendship by providing a catalogued list of our sins on a convenient CD-ROM, but I am suggesting that we should come clean with God. We cannot have true communion with God if we don't relate to Him honestly and openly.

Who do we think we're kidding, anyway, when we hide things from God? He already knows everything we've ever done. He knows things we've long forgotten. The beauty of Jesus' calling is this: Though there is every justifiable reason in creation for there to be a great wall of separation between a holy God and unclean sinners—a wall just as impenetrable as the one between the Jews and Samaritans—Jesus breaks through that wall and asks us for a drink of water. He does this so that we might ask for, and thence He might give us, the living water of an abundant, whole life.

At the end of Jesus' encounter with the Samaritan woman, she ran out of the darkness and into the light. With almost as much exuberance as my nephew Mark, she told everyone in her town that she had met the Messiah, the one they'd been waiting for. The sins and failures of her past were cast off for something far better. They no longer weighed her down and she was now free to tell others about how she had been changed. She was no longer afraid, no longer alone, and no longer ashamed. (After all, the Messiah, who knew everything about her, had even so deigned to talk to her at the well.) And last but not least, as Jesus promised, she was no longer thirsty.

✬ ✬ ✬

*"I have come into the world as a light, so that no one who believes in me should stay in darkness." (John 12:46)*

**Chapter Three: All Shall Be Well**
**Questions for Reflection & Discussion:**

1) Do you agree with Derek Webb's statement that the best thing that could happen to you would be for your sins to be exposed to the world, "broadcast on the five o'clock news"?

2) Take a few minutes to think about your own life. Are there any secrets that keep you in hiding; that keep you from being genuine and honest with other people or with God?

3) What do you think about the author's statement, "Who do we think we're kidding, anyway, when we hide things from God? He already knows everything we've ever done. He knows things we've long forgotten"? Do you find this scary or do you find this comforting? Why?

CHAPTER FOUR

# The Gospel After Dark

Being Born Twice

☆ ☆ ☆

---

# John 3:1-21
# Nicodemus

---

☆ ☆ ☆

**SUGGESTED LISTENING**

Vigilantes of Love: "Double Cure," from *V. O. L.*

Judd & Maggie: "Tired of Wrapping,"
from *Kingdom of Noise*

# The Gospel After Dark
## Being Born Twice

I grew up attending a Christian school, so most of my friends were from Christian homes. I wouldn't say we were all Christians; Christianity isn't inherited, nor is it passed down through one's gene pool. And one certainly doesn't "catch" a true faith from one's friends or the school one attends, as one catches a cold. I wouldn't even say that I was a Christian back then. Still, my friends and I had similar experiences growing up: We attended youth groups, Christian camps, had contemporary Christian music pushed upon us, and knew all the places where dirty words could be found in the Bible.

I had one friend who did not have the same background, though. His name was Kevin.[18] His family was moderately Roman-Catholic and he attended public school. And, despite the lack of Petra, *Superbook*, and Michael W. Smith in his life, he was generally a good kid. Still, because he was my token non-Christian friend, he was always the guy for whom I would pray when the subject of unsaved friends and loved ones came up at youth group or church camp.

---

18 Actually, that's not his real name. It's been changed to protect his privacy.

As I grew older, though, the prayers became more serious. I certainly didn't have all the answers to life's problems and I didn't have everything totally figured out, but I had come to know Jesus, and I wanted Kevin to come to know Him too. Then one day I got a phone call from Kevin. He called to tell me that he had become a Christian. I was shocked. He told me that he had been attending Young Life meetings and had gone away on one of their weekend retreats. There, Kevin had asked Jesus to come into his heart. I was so happy for him, but I don't remember exactly what I said in response to his news. I probably said something like "Congratulations!" because I'd never been taught the socially appropriate response to this kind of news. Moments of burgeoning faith like this one are spectacular, but Hallmark doesn't have a card for the occasion.

As time went by, I envied Kevin. He seemed so on fire for God. He would call and tell me about the things he was learning as he read his Bible. He had invested himself in a local church's youth group, and it seemed like he was always preparing for or getting back from some local ministry opportunity or weekend retreat. Everything he was experiencing was new. For me, this Jesus stuff was old hat. I'd heard the stories before and I knew the songs and I had been a part of the culture for some time. I so wished I could see it through new eyes once again. I wished I could be as excited about the Christian life as Kevin seemed to be.

Then, a couple of months later, Kevin called again. This time he told me that he was no longer a Christian. Once again, I was shocked. I had never known anyone who had walked away from Jesus before. I asked him what happened and he told me that he had been misinformed. He hadn't realized that being a Christian meant giving so many things up. I asked him what things he was being told to give up. He told me that he wanted to have experiences that involved drugs and alcohol and sex. He said if he was going to be a Christian, he couldn't experiment with those things, and to him, that seemed like too much to give up; it seemed as though he would be missing out on something.

It was late at night and the streets were almost empty. Nicodemus walked quickly and quietly. He did not want anyone to see him. When he reached the house where Jesus was staying, he knocked on the door with more force than he intended; he wasn't paying attention to the door because he was busy looking to see if anyone had noticed him.

At first, he had just heard rumors, but then those rumors were confirmed by people Nicodemus trusted. This Jesus, from the little town of Nazareth, an apparently ordinary Galilean carpenter, was anything but ordinary. He had performed miracles. He had healed people of various diseases; He had made a blind man see; He had even turned water into wine. Lately, it seemed that everywhere he went, Nicodemus found himself engaged in conversations about Jesus. *Was he from God? Was he a fraud? What about the friends he keeps? And what should we make of his apparent disregard for the Sabbath regulations?*

Nicodemus hadn't been sure what to make of this Jesus. But then, yesterday, he had heard Jesus teach. Nicodemus was well-versed in the Scriptures—he was a teacher himself—but there was something about the way Jesus taught. It was like nothing he had ever heard before, as if Jesus was able to see the very heart of God in the scrolls of Moses and the Prophets. Jesus told stories that cut to the hearts of His listeners, stripping away their prejudices and preconceived notions. And His ethical instructions! They built upon the Law, but somehow surpassed it. He taught as someone who possessed real authority, not at all like the scribes and rabbis under whom Nicodemus had studied. Nicodemus had become convinced that Jesus was someone special.

The door opened and Nicodemus was taken to an upper room where the teacher was staying. Somehow, Jesus seemed more real in this context. In the temple, He had appeared larger and more powerful. Here in the dark quiet of the evening, there was still a calm dignity in His eyes and a compelling strength in His demeanor, but He was more approachable. Nicodemus had not expected this.

After greeting one another, the two men sat down. Nicodemus said, "Rabbi, we know that you are a teacher who has come from God. For no one could perform the signs you are doing if God were not with him" (John 3:2).

Jesus looked into Nicodemus' eyes. Though Nicodemus had not yet asked a question, Jesus knew why he had come, and why he had chosen the middle of the night for his visit. So Jesus got right to the heart of the matter: "Everyone who sees the kingdom of God has been born twice. You must be born again."

*Born twice?* Nicodemus thought. *How can anyone be born twice? And how did he know that's why I've come?* "But, teacher, what you are saying does not make sense. No one can enter their mother's womb a second time, especially when they are grown. It's nonsense."

Jesus explained that there are two kinds of births: "Flesh gives birth to flesh, but the Spirit gives birth to spirit" (John 3:6). This hardly clarified things for Nicodemus; he was still quite puzzled.

✳ ✳ ✳

Kevin and I drifted apart somewhat during the last half of high school, but we did keep in touch during college. He attended a large, state university in New Hampshire and I went to Gordon College, a Christian liberal arts college near Boston. The schools were about two hours apart, so I invited him to visit me one weekend. I was looking forward to catching up.

Then, the night before he was supposed to come, the phone rang at one-thirty in the morning. I could tell it was Kevin, though it was difficult to hear with all the music and noise in the background. He was clearly at a party, and his speech was slurred; it was obvious he'd been drinking.

"I've been doing some thinking," he said, as though he'd rehearsed what he was going to say before he picked up the phone. He shouted over the party noise, "I'm not coming to visit. I don't need to hear about Jesus or about how I need to be saved or about all the things I do that you don't agree with."

I was stunned. I hadn't said anything about Jesus, and I certainly wasn't planning on confronting Kevin about his life or about the gospel or anything like that. Certainly, if the opportunity came up or he asked about it, I would be ready to tell him that it wasn't too late; that God is all about second chances. But that wasn't why I had invited him. And my campus wasn't any kind of big Billy Graham Crusade either. In fact, on a Saturday afternoon, there probably weren't too many differences between our two schools. I really just wanted to hang out with my old friend. I tried to explain this to Kevin, but he wouldn't listen, and he was not going to change his mind.

The next day, I thought about that conversation and wondered why Kevin was so afraid. He had known me for a long time and I had never tried to force anything on him. I thought about Jesus, though, and what He would think. Should I have tried to talk to Kevin about his drinking or about his drug use? Should I have said something to him about his decision to walk away from Jesus? The last thing I wanted to do was beat him over the head with a Bible. That would have probably just pushed him further away. And, I reminded myself, it wasn't as if I had life all figured out either. I routinely made mistakes. And, though I tried not to, I regularly did stupid things. Who was I to tell him how to live?

Still, there was something strange about Kevin's reaction to my invitation. It was as if he was afraid of the very air he would breathe on Gordon's campus.

✡ ✡ ✡

Nicodemus, too, had been afraid. After all, that's why he had come to Jesus at night. And this fact did not escape Jesus. In His kingdom, though, fear is cast out and there are no secret disciples.

"Do you remember when the Israelites were in the wilderness?" Jesus asked. "Do you remember when God sent snakes to poison the people after they complained against Him?" Nicodemus nodded. Of course he knew the story; he had taught it many times. "Well, if you recall, Moses prayed for the people and the Lord instructed him to make a bronze serpent and put it on a pole for the people to see. Those who lifted their heads up and gazed upon the serpent were healed. The same thing is happening today. The Son of Man must be lifted up, so that all the people who look upon Him can be healed of their disease."

*What disease?* Nicodemus thought, but he'd already embarrassed himself once by not understanding the "born again" thing, so he kept quiet.

Jesus continued, linking to His reference to Moses and the brass serpent by saying, "For God so loved the world that he gave his one and only Son, that whoever believes in him shall not perish but have eternal life. For God did not send his Son into the world to condemn the world, but to save the world through him" (John 3:16-17).

Then Jesus looked again into Nicodemus' eyes, and with a mixture of compassion and concerned insistence, said, "All those who do evil hate the light, and will not come into the light for fear that their deeds will be exposed. But those who live by the truth come into the light, so that it may be seen plainly that what they have done has been done in the sight of God" (John 3:20-21).

Though the Bible doesn't tell us, I imagine that Nicodemus left disheartened that evening. Perhaps he had secretly thought that Jesus would be impressed with him. After all, he was the only member of the Jewish ruling council to visit the young teacher, and by doing so, he was the only one of the group to acknowledge Him, even if it was at night when no one else could know. But instead of being impressed, Jesus told Nicodemus that if he wanted to follow Him, he would have to do so publicly.

After thinking about it for a while, I decided to drive up to Kevin's school. I thought that if I told him I was coming, he would object, fearing I would get all preachy on him. So I decided to surprise him.

I knew what dorm he lived in, so I asked an R.A. in the lobby where I could find his room. She pointed the way and I knocked on the door. A plume of smoke was released as Kevin answered, wearing a T-shirt and boxer shorts. Though it was well after noon, it was obvious that he had not yet left his dorm room that day. He was surprised, but I think he was genuinely happy to see me.

He got dressed and we went to get something to eat. While we ate a greasy late breakfast at a diner just off campus, I thought about what I should say, but I figured the thing Kevin needed most at that point in time was a friend, so I let him steer the conversation. We talked about the classes we were taking, friends we had in common, and the experiences we'd had since starting college. We had a good time together and we laughed a lot. I felt like I made the right choice coming to see him. Still, as I got back in my car a couple of hours later, I was sad. I knew that Kevin needed Jesus more than anything else (as we all do) and I knew that Kevin *knew* he needed Jesus too. But, for some reason, he was not willing to step out into the light and acknowledge Him.

Jesus reminded Nicodemus of the story of the Israelites and the bronze serpent. If you've never heard it before, it may seem a bit odd. The story can be found in Chapter 21 of the book of Numbers, in the Old Testament. The Jewish people were following Moses in the desert and complaining against God, even though He had been faithful and had provided for them at every step in their journey. At one point, God responded to their grumbles by sending venomous snakes to bite the people. That might seem a bit harsh, but God also provided a remedy for the poison—a bronze serpent on a pole. All the people had to do was look up at it and they would be healed. Seems easy enough, right? No co-pay; no deductible; just look at the snake and they would live.

Think about it for a moment, though. Think about being deathly ill and having to crawl out of your tent into the hot air and bright sun of the open desert, all to look at a metal snake on a stick. If I were a sick Israelite, that would have been the last thing I would have wanted to do in such a condition. It had no relation whatsoever to the common wisdom of the day regarding how one recovered from a snake bite. However, looking upon the serpent was a way of acknowledging that God is your only hope. To look up entailed setting aside your pride and recognizing that you couldn't save yourself. All things considered, it was actually quite merciful of God to make it so easy—what if He'd told them to walk ten miles in the desert, climb a mountain, and go into a cave to look at something in order to be healed? Still, because the serpent was on a pole high up in the air, looking at it was a public affair. Everyone could see the decision you had made.

When Jesus told Nicodemus that His followers must leave the darkness and walk in the light, He was inviting Nicodemus to step out into the open. Being a secret disciple just wouldn't work. Like the sick Israelites, Nicodemus needed to make his way into the daytime air—where all could see—and be saved.

I never asked Kevin to step out into the light and be counted, but somehow he knew that Jesus could have no disciples who lived their lives in the darkness. In an odd way, I respect Kevin's decision. He didn't want to be a hypocrite and he knew he wasn't ready to give himself completely over to Jesus. In many ways, I think that's far better than people who give lip service to Jesus, but who secretly live for themselves and love every minute they can spend in that secret darkness.

For Nicodemus, publicly acknowledging Jesus as the Messiah probably would have meant the loss of his position. He was a member of the Sanhedrin, a court that exercised some authority among the Jewish people—one of the only self-governing bodies the Romans allowed the Jews to maintain during that time. Stepping into the light probably also would have meant the scorn of his peers and the loss of the respect and social standing he enjoyed among the people of Jerusalem.

For Kevin, the losses would have been different. He was afraid that by acknowledging Jesus and stepping out into the light, he would be viewed as different from other people. He also thought he would miss out on experiences and things he believed would be fun. Sadly, somewhere along the way, he came to the conclusion that the Christian life is simply a list of things that must be given up; he came to think of Christianity as a life of slavery rather than freedom.

✷ ✷ ✷

I once read an article about a young girl named Macie Hope McCartney. Macie was born again. Now, when I say that she was born again, I don't mean that she had a religious experience or that she came to know Jesus. What I mean is that she was literally born twice.

When Macie Hope was growing in her mother's womb, an ultrasound revealed something else growing—a tumor on the baby's tiny, still-forming body. Though it wasn't cancerous, the tumor was about as big as Macie and certainly would have killed her before she was born. So, six months into the pregnancy, doctors took Macie out of her mother's womb and surgically removed the tumor from her tailbone. Then, the doctors placed her back inside the womb for the duration of the pregnancy. On May 3, 2008, Macie Hope McCartney was born again, healthy as could be.

Macie's story serves as a wonderful illustration of the work that God does when we step out into the light. We are all like Macie in that we need to be born twice.

Being *born again* is another way of saying that when we come to Jesus, we are given a new life. Anyone with a new life full of light does not go back to their old one full of darkness. No, they can walk out of the darkness and into the light because they have nothing to fear. This simply makes sense; the Bible tells us that a life lived in darkness only leads to death, and that the new life is one lived in the freedom of forgiveness and a restored relationship with God. Not only do we gain peace with God, but He goes so far as to adopt us as sons and daughters.

Imagine if Macie had, upon receiving her new life, chosen instead to go back to her old life. Imagine her asking the doctors to surgically reattach the tumor that almost killed her. You're probably thinking, *But who would do that? It doesn't make any sense.* Well, that's just what the Bible says about being born again spiritually. It doesn't make any sense to go back to the old ways. In one of his letters, the apostle John (the same John who wrote the Gospel that bears his name) put it this way: "If we claim to have fellowship with him [God] and yet walk in the darkness, we lie and do not live out the truth. But if we walk in the light, as he is in the light, we have fellowship with one another, and the blood of Jesus, his Son, purifies us from all sin" (1 John 1:6-7).

The only way to follow Jesus is to walk in the light. Walking in darkness is simply not an option for those who have been born again. John tells us that those who try to do so are liars—they're not *really* born again; they're not *really* following Jesus. Walking in the light does not mean that we never sin, nor does it mean that our struggle with sin gets easier overnight. In fact, John says that people who claim to be without sin are also liars (see 1 John 1:8). The only truthful people are those who acknowledge their sin *and* their need of a savior, and who publicly follow Him in the light of day.[19]

---

19 At this point, you may be thinking about the age old question of eternal security: *Is it possible to lose my salvation?* (If you're not thinking this, please feel free to skip this note and save yourself the slight headache that may ensue.) Though the scope of this chapter does not allow for a lengthy discussion on the topic, I'd like to make one observation: After Kevin made the decision to leave the Christian life, there would be two points of view regarding his spiritual standing before God. Those who believe a Christian can lose his salvation would argue that Kevin *had* been saved when he made his commitment to

After Jesus was crucified, Nicodemus was one of the two men who went to Pontius Pilate, the governor, to ask for Jesus' body, so that it could be properly laid to rest according to the Jewish traditions of the time. John's Gospel tells us that Nicodemus and Joseph of Arimathea (another secret disciple who was also a member of the Jewish ruling council) stepped into the light and came forward to be recognized as friends of Jesus. Nicodemus had been afraid to be counted among Jesus' followers before, so he had ventured out at nighttime to meet with Him. Now, he was venturing out at night once again, but this time, he was no longer afraid. This time, he stood in direct opposition to the other Jewish leaders who had fought so hard to put Jesus to death.

John is the only Gospel writer to tell us that Nicodemus went with Joseph to claim Jesus' body. I'm certainly glad that he included that detail. Otherwise, we probably never would have known whether or not Nicodemus took his conversation with Jesus to heart. Maybe his new birth happened during the crucifixion. Maybe, as they were lifting Jesus up on the cross, he remembered the bronze serpent that had been lifted up centuries before, and maybe he called to mind what Jesus had said. Maybe as he gazed upon the cross, he received the healing he needed. And maybe, at that moment, he stepped forward out of the darkness and into the light.

✭ ✭ ✭

*"And I, when I am lifted up from the earth, will draw all people to myself." (John 12:32)*

---

Jesus, but was no longer so after walking away from Him. On the other hand, those who believe in a "once saved, always saved" theology would contend that Kevin was *never* really a Christian to begin with, and the evidence is that he walked away. However, the important thing to note is that, regardless of your particular perspective, both sides would agree that Kevin is presently not a believer... and that is really all that matters, isn't it?

Chapter Four: The Gospel After Dark
Questions for Reflection & Discussion:

1) Read Luke 14:25-35. Jesus compares half-hearted disciples to salt that isn't even fit for the manure pile. What does this tell us about the nature of following Jesus?

2) Think about the story of Kevin that was told in this chapter. Maybe you can relate to his story or maybe you know someone like him. Take a few moments to reflect on your own commitment to Jesus. Is there anything keeping you from following Him completely?

3) What does it mean to "count the cost" of following Jesus? Have you ever personally done so?

# CHAPTER FIVE

# Getting Picked First for Dodgeball

## The Joy of Being Accepted

✲ ✲ ✲

## Luke 19:1-9
## Zacchaeus

✲ ✲ ✲

**SUGGESTED LISTENING**

Eric Peters: "You Can Be Yourself," from *Scarce*

Pierce Pettis: "God Believes In You,"
from *Everything Matters*

# Getting Picked First
# for Dodgeball
## The Joy of Being Accepted

I've never been audited by the IRS before, but I did receive a Letter of Inquiry from the Connecticut Department of Revenue Services (DRS) a few years ago. In the letter, the DRS politely but sternly accused me of trying to defraud the state of its due. They also informed me that I owed $237 in back taxes and $950 in penalties and late fees. Also, though it had taken them two years to find the error, I was being given just over two weeks to fix it.

I frantically rummaged through old papers, tax forms, and pay stubs trying to figure out what I had done wrong. It turned out that since I had moved during the tax year in question and had filed in two states, I had made (what I thought was) a minor mistake. When my Connecticut tax return didn't match my federal filing and my W-2s, the state of Connecticut thought I was trying to get away with something.

Thankfully, I was able to clear up the matter over the phone and I didn't have to pay the insane 400 percent penalty charge; they required only a small late fee. Still, that day I learned that mistakes are not allowed when it comes to taxes. I also learned that there was probably a good reason why tax collectors in the Bible had such a bad reputation.

Time and time again, Jesus was ridiculed for being a friend to tax collectors and sinners, and for sharing meals with them. In some passages, the tax collecting profession is even placed on the same tier with prostitution. In Jesus' day, tax collectors in Israel were considered traitors to their country, since by necessity they worked in such close cooperation with the Roman government. They were also known for being dishonest, often taking more money than the Romans required in order to keep some for themselves. As a result, tax collectors were hated by most people, and Jesus' very association with them was damaging to His reputation.

One of the tax collectors with whom Jesus hung out was a man named Zacchaeus. In Luke's Gospel, we read that he was short of stature. In fact, he was so vertically challenged that when Jesus came to Jericho, walking down the street among crowds of people, Zacchaeus had to climb into a sycamore tree just to get a glimpse of this amazing preacher as he passed by. When Jesus' path crossed that sycamore tree, He stopped. Now, no one would have blamed Jesus if He had just kept on walking. After all, Zacchaeus was known to be a greedy and dishonest man. But Jesus didn't ignore him. Instead, He looked up, and spoke directly and encouragingly to the town's despised tax collector—an act of grace in and of itself. He said, "Zacchaeus, come down immediately. I must stay at your house today" (Luke 19:5). Boy, did this start the crowd buzzing. Not only was He talking to a chief tax collector, but Jesus had even invited Himself to be the houseguest of this notorious sinner.

✳ ✳ ✳

When I was eight years old, my parents divorced. I remember various adults regularly telling me that I shouldn't blame myself for the divorce and that my mom and my dad both still loved me; they just weren't in love with each other anymore. I didn't realize at the time why people kept saying these things. I didn't really ever think the divorce was my fault or that my parents didn't love me. I was more concerned with what the other kids at school might say if they found out my dad wasn't living with us. I'm not sure what I had thought might happen if they found out, but I do recall being afraid of the possibility. I guess I thought it would make me different.

I don't remember everything that happened that year because I think a person's natural tendency is to try to forget bad things. Still, I do recall that during the months following the divorce, my mother spent a lot of time alone. In fact, my sister, brother, and I spent the whole summer at my aunt and uncle's condominium in New York State, just so my mom could work things out. That was okay with me, though, because the condo had a pool.

When we came back home in time for the start of school that September, Mom was still very sad. She didn't want to do much and she cried a lot. Like I said, I don't remember much from that year, but I do remember that my mother stopped getting up with us in the morning. Gone were the days when she would come into our rooms and wake us up, and then make us a big breakfast, all the while making sure we were getting ready for school. When the divorce was finalized, we moved into a smaller house which happened to be right across the street from my school, so I could walk there. Day after day, my sister would make sure I woke up when it was time. Then I'd get myself ready, eat some cereal, and walk across the street to school, all without my mom ever getting out of bed.

The problem was that I was too young to understand that I should care about my appearance. And I had no idea what looked right and what didn't. I mean, eight-year old boys aren't naturally interested in fashion, personal hygiene, or hair care. So when I got up in the morning, I would just don the first shirt and first pair of pants I put my hands on. My outfits didn't always match, and I sometimes forgot to comb my hair and brush my teeth. As a result, I got teased a lot. And since I didn't have anyone to talk to about the teasing, no one taught me how to handle it. So, I just got mad when kids made fun of me, and this made things worse. I found that I had fewer and fewer friends. I was teased so much, I couldn't focus in the classroom and I got sent to the principal's office quite often. Soon, I hated school altogether, and I just stopped doing homework.

As the years went by, I figured some things out and made some friends—some very good ones, actually. But my goal was always simple: just fit in. I never expected to be picked first for dodgeball or to be the smartest kid in any class. And that was okay. I just did my best not to stand out. But even though I was no longer the kid in the corner with his hair sticking up, wearing stripes and plaids together, I still felt like an outcast from time to time.

✵ ✵ ✵

I love the story of Zacchaeus because Jesus makes the first move. Zacchaeus didn't come to Jesus with a list of promises to be better, and Jesus didn't demand anything in exchange for His friendship. Jesus reached out to Zacchaeus while he was still living a sinful life. At no point in the story did Jesus pull out a list of conditions for His love. Instead, Jesus just loved Zacchaeus.

In the movie *Forrest Gump*, Lieutenant Dan, an embittered Vietnam War vet who's lost both legs, takes a generous swig from a liquor bottle and sarcastically asks Forrest, "Have you found Jesus yet, Gump?" With his typical brand of full disclosure, Forrest honestly replies, "I didn't know I was supposed to be looking for him, sir." To Forrest, Jesus had always been there, so there was no need to find Him. Due to his below-average intelligence, he couldn't understand the metaphysical nature of Lieutenant Dan's question, but his response was still unknowingly poignant. It's common to think that we have to find Jesus, as if He's stationary or lost, stuck somewhere and incapable of finding us. But the truth is that Forrest Gump is right. We don't find Jesus; He finds us. And here's the best part: Jesus loves us before we ever do one single thing for Him, no matter how many times we slip and fall—even if our clothes don't match and our hair is sticking straight up.

Jesus told many parables to explain the kingdom of God. In one, He said that the kingdom of God is like a treasure hidden in a field. A man was walking along one day and stumbled across this hidden treasure. He was so overjoyed that he immediately went and sold all of his possessions in order to buy that field and make the treasure his. I've heard this parable many, many times. It's usually explained by saying that Jesus is the treasure and, when we find Him, we ought to give up everything else in life in order to follow Him. That's a beautiful sentiment... except for one thing—I think it's the absolute wrong way to read this parable.

Don't misunderstand me. I think that we should give up anything that hinders us from following Jesus wholeheartedly. However, I don't think that's what Jesus was saying with this parable. It's found in Matthew, Chapter 13, in the midst of many other parables. And here's the thing: In all the other stories in that section, "the man" (the central figure of each parable) is always God—Jesus Himself. So, with that understanding, it's not us finding the treasure that is Jesus; it's Jesus who finds us, and (apparently) considers us a treasure beyond price. But that's not all; the Son of God is so overjoyed by finding this treasure that He empties Himself (sells everything He has) in order to have us with Him forever!

Now, you may ask, *How did Jesus empty himself?* For starters, He left heaven and came to earth to be born into poverty. Then He endured all the messed up things this world has to offer, and He was tempted in every way we were, all without ever sinning. For a finale, He watched as most of His best friends deserted Him. Then He was beaten, tortured, spat upon, humiliated, and killed by being nailed to a Roman cross. All this was done to make a way for you and for me to be with Him forever. All this makes the parable of the treasure hidden in a field one I'll never forget. It kind of puts a different perspective on some of the superficial ways in which we judge one another—stripes and plaids and hair sticking up—doesn't it?

✵ ✵ ✵

When I first arrived at my college, my initial impression was that it seemed enormous (though, truth be told, it's a relatively small school). It wasn't the school's physical size that gave me that impression, though; it was the number of possibilities. Arriving as a freshman, I could be or do anything I wanted. With the exception of one friend with whom I attended high school, no one knew me. College was one giant clean sheet of white paper just waiting to be drawn upon.

After a few weeks, however, reality began to settle in. I couldn't be *anything* I wanted to be. I discovered that I was wired a certain way; all possibilities, therefore, were not equal. And, though I first thought the freedom of a brand-new start would be great, I soon learned that freedom is lonely without friends for the journey. Since I was shy, making new friends was difficult and the first couple of months at college were very lonely.

And then I met Ben Hodges. Before I explain Hodges, let me start by saying that, most of the time, friendship is mutual. Usually, two people encounter each other in some way and they find they share common interests or common concerns. When you're young, that common interest can be something as simple as a love for orange soda. When you're older, the friendship is oftentimes based upon something more substantial than soda (but not always). As far as I could see, there were no shared interests in my friendship with Hodges. And our friendship wasn't mutual… He simply decided that he was going to be my friend. I wasn't consulted.

The day we met, Hodges saw me across a crowded classroom. The professor had not yet arrived, and people were chatting. In his unmistakable Matt-Damon-from-*Good-Will-Hunting* Boston accent, he shouted, "You're in my dorm, right?" At first I assumed his question was meant for someone else and I ignored it, but Hodges was persistent: "Greco, right?" I turned and made polite small talk, and I thought that was going to be it. The next day, however, he showed up in my room just to see what I was doing. For weeks thereafter, he'd show up unannounced just to visit, or he'd find me in the dining hall and invite himself to join me, or he'd just plunk his stuff down next to me in the library and strike up a conversation. Wherever I was, there was Hodges.

To be honest, though, I really didn't mind. It was nice to have someone to talk with. But, at times, it was a bit awkward. We really didn't have much in common on the surface. He was a basketball player, and I have a depth perception problem that makes basketball a laughing matter for anyone watching. He had sworn off secular music because, at the time, he was convinced that Christians should only listen to Christian music, and I was having my ears opened by all the new bands and artists I had discovered since starting college. I kept waiting for Hodges to realize that we really didn't have any common interests. But, as it turned out, our friendship wasn't the serendipitous product of shared concerns. His friendship toward me was an intentional act of pure will. Hodges had simply decided that he was going to be my friend, and there was no avoiding him.

As time went by, our friendship grew. We found we *did* have a lot of things in common. Some of them were silly, and some were important. I made some other great friends at college—friends with whom I'm still close—but to this day, I count Hodges as one of my best friends.

A few years after we graduated, Hodges got engaged to a wonderful woman he had met during college and he asked me to be in the wedding. Since we were living a few hours apart, I drove up the day before the ceremony for the rehearsal and spent the night in the spare bedroom of the condo he'd purchased to share with his new bride. That night I had trouble sleeping, so I began thumbing through a bookshelf looking for something to read. My thumb came across a book with an unmarked spine. Out of curiosity, I pulled the thin volume from the shelf—a black hardcover with some noticeable wear. The cover of the book was also unmarked. Opening it up, I discovered it was Hodges' journal. Up until that moment, I had no idea he had even kept one. I wanted to respect his privacy, so I immediately began closing it up, but not before my eye caught my own name on a page. I couldn't resist, so I began reading.

"For John Greco. I'm not sure what's wrong," was written on the top of one page. "John – help me to be a good friend to him," was written on another. I soon realized that Hodges had scrawled prayer requests at the top of each entry. This journal was from our freshman year at college and my name was on the top of most of the pages. As I flipped through, I saw how he had prayed for me from the beginning of the school year and how he had sensed I was very sad for some reason, though he didn't know why. He wrote about how God kept bringing my name to his mind as he would pray.

As I read, my eyes welled. I had no idea Hodges had been praying for me for so long. And then I began to think about something more amazing. Not only had Hodges been thinking and praying for me, but *God* had been thinking about me too. He had provided me with a good friend when I was desperately lonely—someone with whom I probably would not have become friends under normal circumstances; someone to whom I most certainly wouldn't have reached out. Holding that book in my hand, I felt important to God. He loved me and had been at work behind the scenes without me even knowing it.

✳ ✳ ✳

I imagine that's what Zacchaeus felt like. Up in that tree, all he sought was a glimpse of Jesus. After all, he was a tax collector and a notorious sinner—certainly not someone important enough to bother this important and highly respected teacher. He didn't think Jesus would stop and talk with him, and he certainly didn't expect Jesus to come over for lunch. But

Zacchaeus was important to Jesus, so Jesus showed him undeserved love and acceptance. Like that treasure buried in the field, Jesus spied Zacchaeus up in that tree and sought him out.

But that's not the whole story. During Jesus' visit, Zacchaeus made a startling announcement. He promised to give half of his stuff to the poor. And then he pledged to pay back anyone he may have cheated in the course of his tax-collecting duties *four times* the original amount he had taken. Jesus responded with these words: "Today salvation has come to this house, because this man, too, is a son of Abraham. For the Son of Man came to seek and to save what was lost" (Luke 19:9).

Without being told to give things up, Zacchaeus knew that he could allow nothing to stand between him and Jesus. He became so overjoyed by the fact that Jesus loved and accepted him that the very desires of his heart changed. He was so grateful for his new friendship with Jesus that he was ready to give up a good chunk of his wealth and change the way he performed his tax-collecting duties, becoming fully legitimate. He wanted to be virtuous—right there, in that instant. All it took was some unconditional love.

Zacchaeus' life was now marked by a spirit of tremendous gratitude. Notice that this is completely upside-down from any approach that would have us earn our way to God. Zacchaeus didn't give up his money and strive to be honest so that he could then turn to Jesus and say, "Look, I've done all these things. Now you really have to let me into the club. I've earned your favor and friendship." Instead, while he was still living in sin and before he ever announced his intention to live a transformed life, Zacchaeus felt the sweet, powerful impact of Jesus' friendship. The changed life was made evident by (or, as some Christians might say, "manifested as") an overflow of joy rising up in Zacchaeus' heart.[20] The relationship came first, *then* we see good works as a result, not the other way around. That's just the way God's economy works.

✳ ✳ ✳

The story of Zacchaeus is our story—your story and mine. God longs to meet us where we live, not because of what we've done or how good we are, but on the basis of what Jesus has done on our behalf; on the basis of *His* righteousness. We don't deserve anything—certainly not God's friendship. On our own, the best we can hope for is to see and recognize God's goodness from afar, but there's nothing we can do in our own strength to draw close to Him. That's okay, though. We don't have to rely on our own power or virtue. Jesus came near to us and He's done everything necessary so that we can draw close to Him. A transformed life is what happens when someone *really* meets Jesus. The Son of God comes into that person's life, just like someone entering a home. But just as with a houseguest, Jesus must be welcomed into the house—into that person's life. When that happens, the result is a transformed existence. After all, do you really think it would be possible to spend time with the Son of God and not be changed?

*"But God demonstrates his own love for us in this: While we were still sinners, Christ died for us." (Romans 5:8)*

---

20 Here is another real-world example of what an overflowing life can be. In Zacchaeus' case, he was overflowing with relief and joy—relief at finally being accepted by the One who matters most, and joy, because he was finally operating the way God designed him to. Righteousness is its own reward.

**Chapter Five: Getting Picked First for Dodgeball**
**Questions for Reflection & Discussion:**

1) Could you relate to the author as you read about his childhood experience of feeling rejected? Does knowing that God considers you priceless change the way you view your own experiences?

2) Both the rich young ruler (Chapter Two) and Zacchaeus were wealthy. Why do you suppose Jesus had such different interactions with them?

3) Is there someone in your life to whom God might be calling you to reach out, perhaps in the same way that Ben Hodges reached out to the author during college?

# How to Get High Without Getting Stoned

### Religion Kills

✲ ✲ ✲

## John 8:2-11
## The Woman Caught in Adultery

✲ ✲ ✲

**SUGGESTED LISTENING**

Jon Foreman: "Instead of a Show," from *Summer EP*
Laura Story: "Grace," from *Great God Who Saves*

# How to Get High Without Getting Stoned
## Religion Kills

Rocks hurt. I know this from experience. When I was fourteen, I got hit in the back of the head with a rather large one. My brother James and I were at our dad's house for the weekend. Like a lot of weekends there, my father had a ton of stuff around the house to take care of, so it was up to my brother and me to find something fun to do on our own. In between short stints of helping my dad out with the yard work, we passed the time by tormenting each other. I sprayed him with the hose; he stuffed leaves down my shirt—that sort of thing. No big deal; we were just bored. Neither of us was really being mean. However, as boys are prone to do, it was only a matter of time before one of us took it too far. If it wasn't James, it would've been me. Unfortunately for James, though, it must have been his turn to do something dumb.

From higher ground, he saw me walking up the driveway with the mail in my hand, so he picked up a large rock—about the size of football—and threw it at me. Now, I don't think he actually intended to hit me; I don't think he was that confident in his aim. He just wanted to scare me by having the small boulder hit the driveway close by. But that's not how it turned out.

As I remember it, the world shook violently, but instead of the ground moving, the quaking emanated from my own head. I looked down at the white envelopes I had just retrieved from the mailbox, except they were no longer white. Oddly, they were now red... and wet. Then I noticed that my white T-shirt was also the same curious crimson color. I heard James gasp loudly from somewhere behind me. I turned my head just in time to see him dart around the far side of the house. With the turning motion, blood sprayed over my left shoulder. And then I realized what had happened: I had just been stoned.

I don't know if you can really consider it a stoning if you only get hit by one rock, especially if the thrower never really intended to hit you. Still, after that experience, I have a greater appreciation for anyone in the Bible who's ever been stoned to death. In my book, stoning has got to be one of the worst ways to go. Imagine being taken outside of the city limits of your hometown, being thrown into a pit, and then having rocks—big, sharp, dense, jagged rocks—pelting at you from every direction. The worst part is that there would be no relief. It would be slow and excruciating, but the stones would continue until you were dead and your face and form were no longer recognizable.

✵ ✵ ✵

They knew what Moses had written about adultery. Those ancient words would serve as the perfect test for this new teacher who seemed to have the people of Jerusalem eating out of his hand. With one man on either side, the small crowed briskly marched her into the temple's outer court. When she couldn't keep up, she was dragged along until she picked up her feet and found the pace. Through her tears, she begged them to stop, but in their eyes she was already condemned.

Jesus saw the faction of scribes and Pharisees entering the courtyard with the woman in tow. He had been teaching that morning about God's kingdom. The temple served as the perfect backdrop, for it was there that the people were most aware of God's abiding presence, and it was also there, amidst the sights and sounds of sacrifice, that the people were most aware of their sin. Grace and justice and mercy and judgment were inextricably joined together at the temple. As the mob drew closer, however, Jesus could see that there was no inkling of grace in their hearts, and no real desire for justice in their eyes.

When the small crowd reached the place where Jesus was teaching, the two escorts shoved the woman into the dirt at His feet. Her garments were torn and dirty and her feet had been bloodied from the journey to the temple. Tears of regret still streamed down her face, but she dared not lift her eyes.

"Rabbi, we caught this woman in the very act of adultery, so we've brought her here to you," one of them said.[21] "The Law of Moses demands that she be stoned to death for such a blatant act, but what do *you* say? What shall we do with her?"

Jesus knew what was in their hearts, and that this woman had been brought to Him as a test. Jesus knew the Law better than they did, and He knew this was never its intention. No human being should ever be reduced or humiliated in this way. Because men and women bear God's image, they are extremely valuable. Care should be taken to protect every life, even those which seem to be of less consequence or value in the eyes of society.

---

21 I've always wondered about the other half of that illicit partnership... It's curious how these self-righteous arbiters of God's Law didn't make a citizen's arrest with him, since they witnessed the very act of adultery.

As I sipped my chai tea, I listened to Lucy describe why she didn't like Christians. As a Wiccan, she would never dream of imposing her beliefs on someone else, so she couldn't understand why Christians wanted everyone to be exactly the same. "I think diversity is what makes us beautiful. Wouldn't it be terrible if everyone believed all the same things?" she asked.

I didn't respond. I just listened. There in that small café, things were safe. Divisions weren't necessary; a love of hot, caffeinated beverages was the only requirement for sharing a table and a little bit of conversation. As she continued, she told me about a friend of hers who owned a Wiccan bookstore and how local Christians would regularly disrupt business by shouting hateful things through the front door. Sometimes, they would come in just to create a little bit of disarray, rearranging neatly-shelved books and pamphlets or hiding Christian tracts throughout the store. Lucy told me that her tattoos and her dress often made her a target of ridicule as well. She asked me why Christians were so judgmental.

I was ashamed to be considered part of the same group that had hurt her. I wanted to make a distinction between myself and these people. But it wouldn't have mattered. She knew that I was a Christian and that these things were being done to her and her friends in the name of Jesus.

My next instinct was to try to rationalize what had happened. Perhaps there was a misunderstanding of some kind. But that wouldn't do either. There could be no misinterpreting these actions; they were hateful and judgmental, and there was no way to get around it. When I finally did respond to Lucy's questions, I didn't make excuses for the behavior and I didn't try to explain that I was different than the people who had tried to intimidate her. This wasn't about me. I simply apologized for how she had been treated and told her that the Jesus I had come to know was not like that.

We talked further and I answered some of Lucy's questions about the Bible and what it means to follow Jesus. It turned out that she really was intrigued by Jesus, despite her Wiccan background and the representatives of the Christian faith she had previously encountered. I tried to tell her that Jesus stands ready to forgive, but she wasn't quite yet ready to hear what I had to say. Unlike the woman caught in adultery in John's Gospel, Lucy had not yet come to a place where she knew she needed a savior. She was not yet convicted. My hope is that someday she will be ready to hear the message of the gospel, and that when she is, there will be people ready to graciously point her to Jesus.

When our drinks were gone, Lucy thanked me and told me she wished there were more Christians who would be as open in talking with her. I left the café that morning thinking about Lucy's story and wondering what Jesus would have said to her. As I got into my car, I thought about how many times I might have done or said something insensitive to people who were watching me. It's easy to be religious—to know certain rules from the Bible and practice moral behavior so that others will see that behavior and think well of you—but it can be hard to follow Jesus.

I think Jesus hates religion. That might sound strange at first, but I think it's true, especially if we look at how He handled the religious leaders of His day. Religion is about rules and behavior. It's about separating people into groups—us vs. them. It's about one group of people making a set of rules and imposing those rules upon other people. These rules serve to exclude, to differentiate, and to establish a "hierarchy of the righteous."[22] Jesus' aim was never mere behavior modification and He didn't come to earth to start a new religion. He came to show us all the very heart of God. Rules and doctrinal statements can be helpful, but if you miss out on the most important thing—God's heart—you've gained nothing.

I don't know the Christians who caused Lucy and her friends such distress, but I'm sure they felt their actions were justifiable. Perhaps they thought they were standing up for Jesus by harassing these people who seemed strange and different. But that's religion; that's not following Jesus. And it's really no different than what the scribes and Pharisees were doing with the woman caught in adultery. While their primary aim may have been to trap Jesus, I'm sure they also thought they were honoring God by bringing such a sinner to be punished. Make no mistake; they were very religious.

✵ ✵ ✵

The scribes and the Pharisees had Jesus cornered. If He said the woman should be stoned, the people, who had been so enthralled with all His talk of love and peace, would be quickly disillusioned. Even better for the purposes of these religious leaders, they would have a basis to see that Jesus was arrested. Executions were the sole privilege of Caesar, and anyone who took the law into their own hands was an enemy of the Roman Empire. On the other hand, if Jesus said that the woman should be set free, He would be opposing the Word of God as written in the Law of Moses, which prescribed stoning in the first place. And how could someone sent from heaven—even if they *were* a prophet; even if they were the Messiah Himself—contradict what God had already said? Some of the Jewish leaders

---

22 Religious people like a spirituality that can be easily measured. It's easy to feel good if you measure yourself against other people you've already judged as missing the mark.

concealed a malicious grin as they waited for Jesus to give His answer. They had Him right where they wanted Him.

Jesus, however, did not tremble. He knew what they were up to, and Jesus was no fool. He knew the Law more intimately than any of the scribes or teachers. He knew that His Father in heaven had given the Law to His people because He loved them, and that it was more than just a list of rules to be obeyed. The Law pointed to something much deeper.

While the crowd awaited Jesus' reply, He bent low to the ground and began scrawling letters in the dirt with His finger. The Old Testament records that, when the Law was given to Moses, God etched the Ten Commandments in stone with His finger. Now, in the Person of Jesus, the finger of God was at work again.

The Jewish leaders pressed Jesus for an answer. The crowd waited, wondering if Jesus would be caught in the trap. How would Jesus love these men who faced Him as enemies? And what would become of this woman? Standing up, Jesus responded, "Let any one of you who is without sin be the first to throw a stone at her" (John 8:7). And then Jesus stooped to write in the dirt with His finger for a second time.

Like so many of Jesus' statements, this one seemed to come from another frame of reference—from another world. His words pierced the hearts of those who surrounded the shamed woman; such a response wasn't what the Jewish leaders had expected. Jesus had found a way out of what they thought was a flawlessly designed trap. He hadn't trampled upon the written Law, nor had He forgotten the priorities of God. The Jewish leaders had brought Jesus a religious test, but Jesus wasn't bound by religion. Religion wasn't His concern. That's why

His answer to their question seemed so out of place. Jesus' answer unearthed the true meaning of the Law.

To be sure, the Law was God's standard of perfection, but that standard was never meant to be used as a weapon. That's what religion does. The Law was more than mere religion. It had always pointed to something beyond itself—an immeasurably priceless gift from the heart of Mercy that could never be earned by diligent obedience or impeccable good works.

So, what was Jesus writing in the dirt? No one knows for sure, but some scholars believe that Jesus may have been writing the Ten Commandments. If this is true, perhaps He did so to remind those who were so offended at the woman's adulterous behavior that *no one* had been able to follow the Law flawlessly. As David wrote centuries prior to this event in Psalm 14, verse 3: "There is no one who does good, not even one." Keeping the Law is just not possible. But that's okay; that was never the point. Anyone who alleges that they can keep the Law perfectly is a liar. That was true then and it's true now. Coming to terms with this reality is the first step toward freedom. Only with the knowledge that we cannot please God on our own can the full power of the Law be finally understood, for it is only then that we realize we have no choice but to cry out to God for help. It's only when we give up on religion that we find something far better, and in this we see the true purpose of the Law. But if we refuse to come clean with ourselves and with God, and instead maintain that we can actually justify ourselves before Him, that we (of all people throughout history) are able to keep the Commandments, we stand condemned already. That's what a slavish adherence to religion does; it condemns and judges, while it blinds us to our own sin... and it can *never* set us free.

We were never supposed to put our faith in religion or the Old Testament Law (or in any set of religious rules, for that matter). Our faith is supposed to be placed in God, the Author of the Law. While the Law certainly reveals His holiness, it can also be summed up by a principle founded in love. In fact, the Bible says this: "For the entire law is fulfilled in keeping this one command: 'Love your neighbor as yourself'" (Galatians 5:14).

It is natural to think that a good person loves their friends and hates their enemies. That keeps things simple. People are either in one group or the other. And if you find it difficult to love someone as a friend, then you can just move them into the other group in your mind. Problem solved. Love can be reserved for those who are easy to love or who make it worth your while. However, Jesus said something radical that went far deeper than this natural, "human" kind of love: "But I tell you, love your enemies and pray for those who persecute you" (Matthew 5:44). By saying this, Jesus dissolved the wall between the two groups. There are no longer *friends to be loved* and *enemies to be hated*. Now there is only one group—*people*—and everyone is to be loved.

Think about the guy driving the BMW who cut you off this morning, or the bully in high school that pounded on you just for fun, or maybe it was a parent who left, or a relative who abused you. Jesus wants us to love those people. This life of love is difficult and Jesus didn't sugarcoat this fact. He told would-be disciples that the only way to truly follow him would be to "take up their cross daily" (Luke 9:23).

Sometimes this idea can lose its shocking meaning because it's become a cliché to talk about "carrying your cross." We often hear people flippantly complain about the trivial problems of life by saying, "That's just my cross to bear." When Jesus made this statement, however, the cross was not yet a religious symbol or the badge of any institution. Instead, it was an instrument of torture and death. There were crosses along the roads back then, though not as big as those we drove past in Texas and Oklahoma. In those days, people were stuck up on those crosses, spikes through their hands and feet, dying in agony, crucified by a brutal, imperial power. Such things were a common sight in the Roman Empire, so the original hearers of Jesus' words were familiar with the savage reality of crucifixion. Telling a person to carry their cross daily back then would be like telling someone today to haul an electric chair wherever they went (with the assumption that they would use it on themselves *every day*). It would be like telling them to carry a loaded rifle everywhere they went (with the assumption that they would shoot themselves *every day*). When you think about it that way, it's madness. Who would follow such instructions? Yet, that's the kind of radical life-change Jesus talked about. Dead men don't react or jerk away when you stick them with pins; only when we are dead to ourselves can we be alive to Christ and actually do what Jesus asks us to do. It's the kind of upside-down ethic that makes loving one's enemies possible.

And so, one by one, the scribes and Pharisees walked away from the disgraced, humbled, weeping woman sitting in the dirt. The older men were the first to leave. They had lived long enough to be more fully aware of their own sinfulness. There would be no stones thrown that day. The only stones to be dealt with were in the chests of these men who had become very religious, but who had forgotten about the God who desires not only justice but mercy.

After the Jewish leaders were gone, Jesus turned to the woman and asked her if anyone was left to condemn her. Though there were still tears in her eyes, she looked at Jesus and smiled, shaking her head. Jesus assured her, "I don't condemn you either." The woman had the kind of smile that only comes when someone experiences grace. She knew she was not innocent. What Jesus had done was not justice; it was mercy. She was receiving a pardon. This was a chance to lead a different kind of life, so Jesus directed her to do so: "Go now and leave your life of sin" (John 8:11).

Jesus didn't free this woman from one religion just to be swept up into another. Instead, He offered her a brand-new life. He was able to do this not because the Law didn't matter, and not because He wanted to cut her a break. Jesus could offer this woman a brand-new life because He (not she) earned it.

When the scribes and Pharisees left that day to contemplate their own sin, they were starkly confronted with the ugliness and uncleanness of their lives as God saw them—this is obvious; we see that no one tossed a stone. They, like the woman they caught in sin, needed to be cleansed. There would be no difference between her sin and their sin on the Day of Judgment, unless, of course, something could be done about their unholy condition. Religion doesn't work, because it does nothing to change the heart.

Without getting too theological, let me try to explain how Jesus was able to grant a pardon to the adulterous woman, and how, if the scribes and Pharisees ever turned to Him, He could offer them the same new life. When Jesus lived on earth, He was fully God and yet fully human. As a human, Jesus had to keep the Law in its entirety in order to fulfill His role as God's perfect Sacrifice for the sins of all human beings throughout history. And He did so; Jesus never sinned. When Jesus died on the cross, the sins of the world were placed upon Him and He took the punishment for you and for me; for the woman caught in adultery, and for the scribes and the Pharisees. His sacrifice was acceptable to God because He Himself was without sin.

When someone turns to Jesus in faith, an amazing thing happens. God no longer sees the ugliness of their sins. Instead, He sees the perfect life that Jesus lived on their behalf. Justice no longer demands that we be separated from God for eternity because of our sin. Our debt to God has been paid by Jesus' death on the cross. In this sense, Jesus was perfectly religious *so we don't have to be*.[23] He kept the Law perfectly. Then, He took the penalty for not keeping the Law perfectly—the penalty that every one of us deserves—upon Himself.[24]

As I mentioned, the scene with the woman caught in adultery took place at the temple. As the men around her debated her fate, I wonder if this woman heard the sounds of the animals waiting to be sacrificed. I wonder if she thought about how her fate could've been the same as theirs—an ugly, bloody death because of sin. And I wonder if she was in Jerusalem some time later when Jesus was crucified. Did she then realize that Jesus was the spotless Lamb who had to be sacrificed for her sins? Did she realize how costly it was for Jesus to say, "Neither do I condemn you" (John 8:11)? I'd like to think that as she lived her new life, bought at such a great price, she turned from her old

23 Please don't misunderstand, though. We don't have to keep the Law perfectly, because we can't. And God is not some unreasonable taskmaster. Instead, in His graciousness, He provided the perfect substitute to keep it flawlessly on our behalf. But this does not mean that there's no value in obedience. In fact, nothing could be further from the truth. As we come to know Jesus in a relationship, our love for Him pushes us to want to do the things He did, to be like Him, and to please Him as He pleased the Father. We should never say, "Well, since I don't have to be religious, I can just do what I want, and God will accept me anyway." At the same time, our desire for righteousness should burst forth out of our love for Jesus, rather than from some misguided attempt to justify ourselves.

24 This brief summary of what is often called *substitutionary atonement* is not meant to negate or ignore other views of the atonement doctrine. If you're interested in a more thorough and scholarly discussion of various (but not necessarily conflicting) viewpoints related to the issue of Christ's sacrificial death, check out James Beilby and Paul R. Eddy, eds., *The Nature of the Atonement: Four Views* (IVP Academic, 2006).

pattern of sin and guilt to a life of love lived out of gratefulness for the One who had set her free.

*"Therefore, there is now no condemnation for those who are in Christ Jesus, because through Christ Jesus the law of the Spirit who gives life has set you free from the law of sin and death." (Romans 8:1-2)*

**Chapter Six: How to Get High Without Getting Stoned**
**Questions for Reflection & Discussion:**

1) What would you tell Lucy if given the opportunity to sit down and talk with her?

2) In the story of the woman caught in adultery, do you identify more with the woman or with the men who brought her to Jesus? Why?

3) Have you ever thought about what it means to "carry your cross daily"? What might that look like in your own life?

CHAPTER SEVEN

# Go and Do Likewise

Love Grows from the Inside Out

✡ ✡ ✡

## Luke 10:25-37

**A Lawyer (The Parable of the Good Samaritan)**

✡ ✡ ✡

**SUGGESTED LISTENING**

David Crowder Band: "A Beautiful Collision (B Variant)," from *B Collision*

Andy Gullahorn: "That Guy," from *Reinventing the Wheel*

# Go and Do Likewise
## Love Grows from the Inside Out

I think we may have lost something very special. I think we may have lost our stories. If you read through the Gospels, you'll notice that Jesus told lots of stories, commonly referred to as *parables*. Rarely did He communicate using simple platitudes or static value statements. Instead, Jesus talked about lost sheep, lost coins, and lost sons. He told folks about mustard seeds and hidden treasures. He related parables about sowing fields, building towers, and investing money. Jesus communicated truth without rigid doctrinal statements or theology textbooks. Jesus was a master storyteller.

Even when teaching the ethics of the kingdom, His lessons were colorful. He explained things using situations His listeners could relate to their daily lives. Jesus talked about turning the other cheek, walking the extra mile, and leaving your offering at the altar in order to go and make amends with your brother. Jesus didn't simply say, "Lust is wrong." Instead, he talked about the need to gouge out your eye or cut off your hand if lust is a problem. This was, of course, not a literal command, but rather a vivid illustration of the destructive nature of sexual sin, and how seriously we should go about taking steps to avoid it. Each of His word-pictures had significant meaning in the culture wherein they were spoken. I doubt if anyone who heard His messages forgot them.

This emphasis on story is reflected throughout the pages of the Bible, which is itself a diverse document. It was written by dozens of people from an array of backgrounds, living on three continents, over a period of more than a thousand years. Even with all that variety, the Bible itself is a singular story. Yes, there are laws and there are letters. There is poetry and there is prophecy. The library of Scripture contains a myriad of genres, but, taken as a whole, the Bible is one grand story, and even the non-narrative parts contribute a great deal to the larger tale of redemption.

So, if the Word of God is a story, and Jesus Himself loved stories, Christians ought to be a people known for their stories. After all, Jesus proved that stories are far more powerful than simply having all the right answers (not that any of us can claim to have all of them). Stories illuminate and speak to a person's soul in a way mere orthodoxy or religious instruction never can.

Take, for example, the account of a lawyer who asked Jesus, "What must I do to inherit eternal life?" (Luke 10:25). When I read these words, I can't help but think that this is just the sort of question one would expect a lawyer to ask. He didn't want to know about the heart of God, he didn't ask ethical questions, and he didn't want to debate the finer points of theology. He just wanted to know how to get eternal life—he wanted to know what he needed to do to get into heaven. He wanted to be prepared for Judgment Day, and he wanted to make sure that there wouldn't be some unexpected loophole that would cost him his eternal reward.

Jesus loves everyone (even lawyers), so He responded in a way a lawyer could best understand. He engaged him in a discussion about the Law itself. "What is written in the Law? How do you read it?" Jesus asked.

This legal expert was apparently no slouch and came prepared with his best understanding of God's Word. In response to Jesus' question, he quoted a pair of verses from the Old Testament: "'Love the Lord your God with all your heart and with all your soul and with all your strength and with all your mind'; and, 'Love your neighbor as yourself'" (Luke 10:27; cf. Deuteronomy 6:5 and Leviticus 19:18).

Without phoning a friend or asking the audience, the lawyer answered correctly. And, to his credit, he appears to have been on the same page as Jesus. In fact, these two commands are precisely how Jesus had summed up the Law on another occasion, and so Jesus tells the man that he answered correctly. "Do this and you will live" (Luke 10:28), the Son of God says, echoing the promises of life given in the Old Testament for those who kept the same commands. Still, this was not good enough for the lawyer (Luke actually tells us that the lawyer wanted to justify himself), so as lawyers are prone to do, he pressed Jesus for specifics, asking, "And who is my neighbor?" (Luke 10:29).

Here's where the storytelling comes in. Jesus understood that He had to get at this lawyer's heart. For a truth to really stick in a person's soul, it needs to cut deep, through any defensive armor or protective mask they might be wearing. Stories are a gentle and effective way to do this. So Jesus told the lawyer a story about highway robbery and a savage beating. A man had been traveling from Jerusalem to Jericho. On the way, he encountered brutal thieves. They beat the man half-dead, stripped him of his possessions and his clothes, and more importantly, his dignity. Over the course of time, three men passed by the spot where the man was lying in dire need. The first was a priest; the second was a Levite. In that culture and at that time, both men would have been recognized as people who were supposed to be dedicated to God's service, yet they passed by on the other side of the road, ignoring the obvious need of the poor robbery victim.[25] The last man to come upon the scene was a Samaritan—someone the Jews would have viewed as "unclean" and most assuredly outside of God's plans or concerns. This Samaritan, however, stopped and cared for the ailing traveler, bandaging his wounds and carrying him to shelter at a nearby inn. He assumed the burden of financial responsibility for the injured man's care, leaving money with the innkeeper in case of additional expenses.

After telling this story, Jesus turned to the lawyer and asked, "Which of these three do you think was a neighbor to the man who fell into the hands of robbers?" (Luke 10:36). The lawyer had no choice but to admit that the Samaritan had acted more like a neighbor than the other two who had avoided the situation altogether. The priest and the Levite would have been considered upstanding Jews in the eyes of the community, but the Samaritan had proved to be the only one who truly understood the concerns of God. Jesus had pricked the lawyer's heart. Salvation was not about following a set of rules, but about

---

25 I recently saw a video on the local news in which an elderly man was run down by a speeding car while trying to cross the street. The driver of the car sped off, apparently without a second thought about the man he may have just killed. But that wasn't the most shocking thing in the video. This incident happened in a crowded city. There were dozens of people nearby, many of whom witnessed the hit-and-run as it took place, yet no one ventured to help the poor man lying in the middle of the crosswalk, and no one pulled out a cell phone to call an ambulance. Cars drove around the man in the street; people stared for a moment and then moved on. For a full two minutes, people just went about their business, ignoring the tragic scene as best they could. We might read the parable of the Good Samaritan and think that only the coldest of people could behave like the priest or the Levite in the story, but the only thing that separates them from the folks I saw on the news was the traffic camera.

following the heart of God. And so, Jesus instructed him, "Go and do likewise" (Luke 10:37).

A few years ago, I was serving on the Christian Guidance staff of the Billy Graham Evangelistic Association. While in that job, I worked as an usher during the dedication of the Billy Graham Library. Though working that day meant getting to the Billy Graham headquarters by five o'clock a.m., enduring a fourteen-hour day, and sweating through my suit in the 98-degree North Carolina heat and humidity, it was worth it to be a part of such an historic event. The dedication was one of Billy Graham's last public appearances, and he was joined on stage by three former presidents: Jimmy Carter, George H. W. Bush, and Bill Clinton. Since I was working as an usher to the first section of seats right in front of the stage, I had the good fortune to be as close to the presidents as one could be without being signed up for the Secret Service.

It has been said that Billy Graham has preached the gospel to more people in person and on television than anyone else in human history. In the course of his storied life, he's become good friends with a myriad of celebrities and world leaders, including every president from Harry S. Truman to George W. Bush. So it was fitting that the three living ex-presidents at the time of the library dedication came to honor Mr. Graham.

Of all the speeches that day, President Clinton's speech will stay with me the longest. To understand why, realize that I grew up in the Christian subculture of the 1980s and '90s. In those days, it seemed to me that Jesus was a tried-and-true Republican. It might never have been stated in such terms, but every God-fearing Christian I knew was a Republican, and the expectation was that anyone with an interest in the things of

God would also be a supporter of the GOP. It now seems reckless to have reduced God's influence to one political party, but fear can be a powerful force.

I can remember a mock election we had at my conservative Christian high school in 1992. We had George H. W. Bush beating Bill Clinton with 98 percent of the vote (with a 2 percent margin of error). This brand of political polarization was just part of the air one breathed in the Evangelical Christian subculture of the time. Democrats, and especially the Clintons, were bad news. It wasn't just social and moral issues like homosexual rights and abortion that got people fired up, either. I'm ashamed to admit that most of us hated Bill Clinton personally. After the Monica Lewinsky affair, he *really* became the enemy. Looking back, it's hard to believe that I didn't notice the inconsistency between the way that I and other folks had demonized Bill Clinton and Jesus' command that we ought to love our enemies. It had never even crossed my mind that our response to him should be one of love.

I think Bill Clinton came to the Billy Graham Library dedication, not as a former president, and not even as a personal friend of Mr. Graham's, but simply to share the impact Billy Graham had made on his life. In his speech that day, Bill Clinton reflected on that impact, which began at the 1959 Billy Graham Crusade in Little Rock, Arkansas. Though he was only a boy, Bill Clinton was there, watching as Billy Graham made a bold statement against segregation. The community had wanted the evangelistic meeting to be for whites only, but Mr. Graham refused to come unless the event was open to all people, regardless of color. He could've accepted this racism as just a sad fact of life and not gotten involved, but Billy Graham understood that the heart of God beats for the poor and the oppressed—for people who are in need, and for those who seem to be of little importance.

Mr. Clinton also shared something about that crusade that most people never would have known. In the days leading up to the meeting, Mr. Graham took time out of his busy schedule to visit with Bill Clinton's bed-ridden pastor. So, as a boy, Bill Clinton got to listen to Billy Graham encourage and pray for his sick minister. He got to hear about eternity and the wonderful promises of God. And he got to see what it looks like when someone takes on the ethic of the Good Samaritan. Noticeably choked up, Bill Clinton said this during his speech at the library dedication: "In the Scripture, Jesus tells us that the most important commandment is to love God with all our heart and then He said that the second is—quote—like unto it: to love your neighbor as yourself—unquote. I have seen [Mr. Graham] do that in private, when no one was looking."[26]

At first glance, one might conclude that the lesson being taught by the parable of the Good Samaritan is that good people go to heaven and bad people don't. After all, the story was prompted by the lawyer asking how he could attain eternal life. He was looking for something he could *do*—an activity or a behavior that would secure his place in God's kingdom. But that's not what Jesus' story was really all about. Being a Christian isn't about what we do or don't do. It's not about voting a certain way or assenting to certain truths. It's about being changed by Jesus through a relationship with Him. The Good Samaritan embodied this changed life. His actions were not a

---

26 William Jefferson Clinton, speech given at the Billy Graham Library Dedication Ceremony, May 31, 2007 in Charlotte, NC. Video clips from the ceremony, including the quotation above, are available online at: http://www.billygraham.org/mediaplayer.asp.

mere checklist to prove his righteousness; they were instead the generous result of a life surrendered to God.

Everyone knows that Billy Graham is a wonderful Christian. That's nothing new. But here's the incredibly radical thing: We can all be just like Billy Graham. Why is this true? Because Billy Graham's secret to living an extraordinary life isn't a secret at all. Early on in his ministry, he simply made the decision that his goal would not be fame, wealth, or power. Instead, it would be to try and exemplify Jesus in his words and his actions—both in public and in private.

That's what the story of the Good Samaritan is all about. The most remarkable thing about the Samaritan was that he could've gotten away with doing nothing. Like the priest and the Levite that came before him, the Samaritan could've crossed to the opposite side of the road and no one would have known. And that was certainly part of Jesus' message to the lawyer who prompted the story in the first place. Lawyers are concerned with laws—what we can and cannot get away with. Yet following Jesus is not about figuring out what's permissible and what's not. It's about becoming a new creation. It's about becoming someone who doesn't look to see if anyone will notice a good deed. If you aren't becoming a new creation—if you aren't seeing your life steadily changing from the inside out—then are you really following Him?

✵ ✵ ✵

The Bible doesn't tell us much about the lawyer—not even his name—but we do know that he was quite astute. He was able to glean the truth about God's heart from his careful reading of the Old Testament Law. One thing still bothered him, though, and he needed clarification. He was perplexed about who his neighbor might be. I imagine that Jesus' answer must have been quite shocking. After all, I'm sure he was looking to narrow down the definition of *neighbor* rather than expand it. But expand it is exactly what Jesus did. With the story of the Good Samaritan, Jesus forever defined a *neighbor* (the folks we are to love, second only to God) as anyone we meet on our way through this life.

I will readily admit that it's not easy to live this way. But I think I could probably do it if everyone else would just get on board with all this loving-our-enemies and turning-the-other-cheek business first. Imagine a world like that. Envision rush hour traffic without getting cut off or having an SUV riding on your bumper just because you don't want to double the speed limit. Think about a workplace where people are the priority, rather than the bottom line. Think about a family where each member is concerned about the welfare of the others. In that world, it would be easy to love everyone. But life doesn't flow that way, does it? And it's hard to go against the current; it's no picnic to be the first one to respond with love. Looking at it objectively, it seems nearly impossible to be transformed into someone whose life is nothing short of a revolution, but that's precisely the kind of life to which Jesus calls us.

Toward the end of His earthly ministry, hours before Jesus was arrested, He shared some final lessons with His disciples. One was about the power necessary to live the kind of life I've been describing in this chapter. With another word-picture, Jesus explained that, apart from Him, none of us can do the kind of good works that mark an extraordinary life. He compared Himself to a vine and His followers to branches growing in a vineyard. Then He said, "If you remain in me and I in you, you will bear much fruit; apart from me you can do nothing" (John 15:5). The secret to living like the Good Samaritan is to stay connected with Jesus. Without that connection, we *will* fail; swim as hard as we like, we will eventually end up drifting downstream with the current of the world. Our hearts will never truly share the concerns of God's heart if we're not living intimately with Him from day to day.

Growing up as an Evangelical and a de facto Republican, I remember hearing how Bill Clinton didn't believe the same things we believed—that he was one of the people responsible for "turning our nation away from God." He was someone to blame, though he should have been someone to love. We should have seen Bill Clinton, not only as the president God ordained for our nation, but as an opportunity to practice being Good Samaritans. After all, what matters most is not the *object* of our love and kindness, but the *Source* of the love we have to give.

*"And so we know and rely on the love God has for us. God is love. Whoever lives in love lives in God, and God in them." (1 John 4:16)*

**Chapter Seven: Go and Do Likewise**
**Questions for Reflection & Discussion:**

1) In John 13:35, Jesus made this statement: "By this everyone will know that you are my disciples, if you love one another." If you're a Christ-follower, take a moment to consider this statement. Does your daily life reflect this kind of love?

2) Do you think Christians are known *primarily* for the love they show each other and the rest of the world? If not, what do you think Christians are known for?

3) How does Jesus' definition of *neighbor* affect the way we are to live our lives, specifically in light of God's command that we love our neighbors as ourselves?

CHAPTER EIGHT

# The Most Important Question Ever Asked

## Coming Face to Face with Reality

✲ ✲ ✲

## John 18:28-19:16
## Pontius Pilate

✲ ✲ ✲

**SUGGESTED LISTENING**

Ten Shekel Shirt: "Poorest King," from *Risk*

Jason Harrod: "When I Fly Away," from *Bright as You*

# The Most Important Question Ever Asked
## Coming Face to Face with Reality

When I was in high school, I went to Jamaica for ten days. In a vote as hotly contested as the 2000 presidential election, my senior class decided to forego the traditional class trip to Walt Disney World in favor of a missions trip to Jamaica.

Regardless of what you may have seen on TV, the interior of Jamaica is nothing like the commercials showing coastal resort towns and gobs of tourist attractions. We did not experience the pristine, private beaches, and we didn't visit the award-winning golf courses. The country we saw was very rural and very poor.

On our way to the Bethel Christian Mission, our bus zigged and zagged up mountain roads. I'm pretty sure that we came barely inches from careening off the dirt road and into a deep ravine more than a few times. When we arrived at the mission, we were met by something I had not expected—hundreds of white teeth. Dozens of children from the area had seen our bus coming up the mountain and came to greet us with big, beautiful smiles.

After unpacking, my friend Ross and I spotted some kids playing soccer in an overgrown field behind the mission, so we went out to join them. As we got closer, we noticed something strange. The kids didn't have shoes. There they were kicking a fully inflated soccer ball barefoot while running on uneven, rocky ground. When we asked if their feet hurt, they just smiled and laughed a bit. Later, we found out that many of those children had never owned a pair of shoes, so their feet were hard, rough, and calloused. They didn't mind kicking a hard soccer ball or running on rocks, because they couldn't feel the pain. On closer inspection, it appeared some of their feet were even misshapen. Ross and I looked down at our brand-new Nikes. Then we looked at each other, silently sharing the thought that maybe we should take them off.

The next day, we began work on a construction project. I hauled cinder blocks back and forth from one site to another for about three hours, but it seemed more like thirty. We were building a house for a homeless family. I say it was a house, but if you would've seen it, you would have thought it was more like a tool shed. It was just four walls of cinderblock covered with a flat metal roof and ventilated by a couple of windows. Through the sweat that was running into my eyes, I could see big white teeth once again; the new homeowners beamed with joy.

After the construction project, the full-time missionary we were staying with, Rick, took a few of us to visit a woman named Mary. Mary was in her nineties and lived alone; the rest of her family had passed away. Rick checked on her several times a week, bringing her food and occasionally a doctor. Her house was even smaller than the tiny cinderblock project we were building. There was, of course, no electricity and the windows weren't actually windows—just holes in the wall where cinderblocks had been omitted. The gaps weren't very large, so they let in only a small amount of light. Mary's house had one room and she was lying on a cot when we arrived. As we slowly filled the room, she pushed herself up against the wall by her bed, taking us all in. I had never seen someone so thin. But there it was again: a big, beautiful smile.

Rick gave Mary a Tupperware bowl with some stew, and though she must have been hungry, she put it aside. She had visitors at the moment, and would have plenty of time for eating when she was alone again. She had one thing on her mind: She wanted to sing, and she would not miss an opportunity to sing with other people. She started calling out hymn titles like "Amazing Grace" and "O, For a Thousand Tongues to Sing" and asking if we knew them, never pausing long enough to hear us answer before shouting out another title. She was so excited.

As we began the second verse of "Amazing Grace," I thought about how backward this situation seemed. Here was this incredibly poor, incredibly old woman with no money or family, and her greatest desire was to sing to God with people she had just met. We were rich and well fed, and before this trip, I could've listed dozens of things I "needed." Now they all seemed like garbage, like things in the way of the one thing I really needed. Mary had that one thing. She was the richest person I'd ever met.

✵ ✵ ✵

For Pontius Pilate, mornings always seemed to come too soon. It was bad enough being assigned to govern a tiny district on the outskirts of the empire, so far away from the city of Rome, but these headstrong, unrelenting people hardly gave him a moment's rest. If it wasn't an outright revolt, it was some obscure religious dispute that had the crowds foaming at the mouth and bellowing in the streets. It wasn't that he had a problem squashing unrest. It was just that, no matter the cause, every incident reflected poorly on his ability to govern.

But here it was, barely past sunrise, and there was already shouting and banging outside the palace walls. And last night had not been a good night. Pilate's wife woke him constantly with her tossing and turning. She often suffered from nightmares, and last night she'd seemed especially tormented.

As he left his chambers to see what all the commotion was about, a servant met him in the hall to tell him that some of the Jewish leaders had brought a prisoner, Jesus of Nazareth. *Couldn't this wait?* Pilate thought. *What could be so important so early in the morning?*

Then Pilate remembered that this weekend was one of those blasted Jewish festivals, one that brought people from far and wide. This was, of course, good for trade, but it was also incredibly dangerous. If there were to be riots with so many people in Jerusalem, it was sure to be noticed by Rome. *Better if the Jews bring any troublemakers directly to me before things get out of control*, he reasoned.

His guards brought in the cause of the commotion. Pilate was underwhelmed and furrowed his brow in confusion. *This...? This is the reason for shouting at six in the morning?* The prisoner was not much to look at. He was unkempt, poorly dressed, and sporting a fresh bruise on his cheek. He was pathetic, but in no way did the prisoner appear to be dangerous. Still, there was something about the way the man looked at him; Pilate could feel his very soul being pierced. The day wasn't getting any better.

As Pilate went out to the balcony to hear the accusations against this man, he breathed a sigh of relief. *This should be over rather quickly. This prisoner hardly looks as though he could be guilty of anything too serious.*

"What charges do you bring against this man?" he shouted at the tumultuous crowd who remained outside, refusing to cross the entryway of his property. Pilate had always felt a little insulted that these Jewish leaders—priests and scribes mostly— considered him and his household to be "unclean." However, he quite enjoyed looking down upon the masses from his veranda. It was, after all, a perfect picture of the way things really were. They were his subjects—slaves, really—and he possessed immense power over every aspect of their lives.

"If he were not a criminal... we would not have handed him over to you" (John 18:30), they replied, shaking their fists in anger.

At this, Pilate became frustrated. *If they can't even name a crime he's committed, why are these Jews wasting my time?* He replied firmly, "Take him yourselves and judge him by your own law" (John 18:31). Pilate then turned away from the balcony's edge.

Some of the leaders in the now-boiling crowd shouted back in response, "But we do not have permission to put a man to death!" Upon hearing this, Pilate stopped in his tracks. *This was no trivial matter.* There was now no question as to why the large crowd had gathered outside his palace. They wanted blood. The last thing Pilate wanted was another incident of civil unrest, so this situation would have to be handled very delicately and very quickly.

Turning back toward the crowd once more, he asked insistently, "But what has this man done?"

"This man is an enemy of the state!" they shouted. "He instructs people not to pay their taxes, and even opposes Caesar by claiming to be a king!"

*Since when have these Jews ever shown loyalty to Caesar?* he thought. Returning to the hall, he looked Jesus over once again. *He's not a very convincing king.* "Tell me who you are, prisoner. Are you the king of the Jews?" Pilate asked.

"Is that your own idea," Jesus asked, "or did others talk to you about me?" (John 18:34).

"What has this to do with me? Am I a Jew?" Pilate responded. Again, he was surprised by the calm in Jesus' eyes. These were not the eyes of a crazed religious zealot or violent insurrectionist. "Look! You must have done something to upset the priests and all these people. Tell me what it is you've done."

Jesus said, "My kingdom is not of this world. If it were, my servants would fight to prevent my arrest by the Jewish leaders. But now my kingdom is from another place" (John 18:36).

"So you admit it, then? You do claim to be a king!" Pilate responded, finally feeling as though he was getting somewhere in this infuriating situation.

Jesus answered, "You say that I am a king. In fact, the reason I was born and came into the world is to testify to the truth. Everyone on the side of truth listens to me" (John 18:37).

And that's when it happened. Without realizing it, Pontius Pilate asked the most important question ever asked in all of human history.

"What is truth?" (John 18:38).

✷ ✷ ✷

*What is truth?* On this question, all history hinges. Is the true nature of reality found in what the Romans were telling people? Does peace and security lie in conquest and military might? And the Jewish leaders—was their truth *true*? Do we please God by obeying laws and keeping ceremonially clean?

Or is the truth asserted by this peasant carpenter the *real* truth? Is He *really* the king of an unseen kingdom, one which will never end, one in which there is no hunger, poverty, pain or disease? Does God really love us and long to welcome us home as a father welcomes a prodigal child? *What is the truth?*

The answer to this question has the power to pull the deep reality of God's kingdom from the shadows of the unseen out into the sunlight. I think Mary and the other people we met in Jamaica had asked the question and received the answer. And when they received the answer, they believed it with all their hearts. They knew more about the true nature of reality than did my classmates and I. While we were worried about trifling things, these people had very real needs. Yet they had overflowing joy, and we were the ones who grumbled and complained. To any onlooker, we were rich and they were poor. We were blessed and they were not. But that's the funny thing about this kingdom business: Appearances aren't everything. Though it may have looked like we were standing in the cinderblock hut of an old, sick Jamaican woman, cheering her up with familiar songs, in kingdom terms, we had been invited to a palace to join a daughter of the King of the Universe in worship.

I don't mean to trivialize the plight of the poor. Mary and people like her are suffering physically, and they have real needs that must be met. However, there is also a deeper truth… and Mary found it. This truth didn't change her poverty instantly, and knowing that someday hunger would be a thing of the past didn't bring that day any nearer. But living every day in the very truth of the kingdom *did* change Mary's perspective, and it *did* bring her hope. Reality is now different for Mary and the others we met in Jamaica, as well as for countless Christians throughout the world who've embraced the truth of the kingdom. But, again, the change is like the kingdom itself: Most people cannot see it.

Jesus once described the kingdom of God as a mustard seed. A mustard seed is as small as anything that existed in Israel at that time—almost too small to see. Still, within that seed is everything needed to produce a tree so large that the birds of the air can find rest in its branches. When we receive a glimpse into the true nature of reality (what Jesus often called the *kingdom of God*), it's like that seed. The large tree it contains within is completely hidden, but it's there; it's just not grown. And the seed itself is the only evidence of the tree's existence.

Maybe it's easier for poor people to embrace hope. After all, a seed means more to someone with no trees at all than to those who live in a forest. It can be hard for us to see what the big deal is. And didn't Jesus say, "Blessed are you who are poor, for yours is the kingdom of God" (Luke 6:20)? Mary beams and dances and holds the seed as if it's the most precious thing in the Universe, while we look on in disbelief, not understanding what's so great about an insignificant little mustard seed. But that's only because we don't really understand mustard seeds.

Finding the truth should change the way we look at the world, but it should also change the way we live. And that's what makes Jesus so dangerous. He came declaring that God loves us and that we can't earn His favor. He came teaching that God's kingdom is unlike the kingdoms of this world. But most importantly, He came to tell us that God wants to have an intimate relationship with each of us. This is a radically different reality than most of us expected. Still, once we are confronted with the truth, we must make a choice. We must accept the truth and live our lives in light of it, or we must reject it and continue walking in darkness, pretending that we never heard the truth at all. Once the truth gets in your face, though, there is no going back to life the way it was—you can try to pretend, but things will never be the same.

✳ ✳ ✳

Pilate tried to pretend. He tried to put off dealing with Jesus. Returning to the Jewish leaders and common people who had gathered outside his home, he thought of a way to please the crowds *and* clear up this potentially disastrous sociopolitical crisis.

"I can find nothing that would amount to a charge against this man," Pilate said. "However, as it is your custom to have me pardon one prisoner during the Passover celebration, why don't I release this 'king' of yours?" Pilate thought of the violent men he had locked up recently for theft and murder, some of whom had even committed treason. *Surely, in comparison with those criminals, this Jesus of Nazareth would be worthy of amnesty.*

"No! Give us Barabbas!"

Pilate remembered Barabbas. He was one of the worst. He was a murderer and a thief, someone who surely deserved death by Jewish *or* Roman standards. *If they'd rather have Barabbas back on the streets instead of Jesus, this situation is more serious than I first thought.*

Still, Pilate remembered that he was ultimately in charge. No one would be put to death without his authorization. "Take the prisoner and have him flogged," he ordered a nearby soldier. He didn't want to go out into the hall himself. He didn't want to face those piercing eyes again.

Some time later, after Jesus had been humiliated and beaten bloody, He was brought out to face the crowd. Pilate could see that the soldiers had had some fun with Him. They paraded

Him out wearing a purple robe and a crown of thorns, and, one by one, they mockingly bowed down before Him. *Still*, Pilate thought, *better bloody than dead*.

The Roman governor shouted to the crowd, "Look, I am bringing him out to you to let you know that I find no basis for a charge against him" (John 19:4). *Surely, once they see how badly he's been beaten, their rage will be satiated.*

But the beating wasn't enough. The angry crowd shouted all the louder, "Crucify! Crucify!" (John 19:6).

Pilate stood his ground: "I told you; I find no evidence to charge him with a crime!" The anxiety in his voice grew. *What was it about this man? Why does he have the people so filled with hate? And why can't I look him in the eye?*

But the chief priests responded, "We have a law, and according to that law he must die, because he claimed to be the Son of God" (John 19:7).

*The Son of God!* Pilate trembled when he heard this. *Who was this prisoner? He can't possibly be telling the truth, could he? But why are the people so set against him? Crazy people are pitied, mocked, locked up, but not crucified by an angry mob.* Turning to Jesus, he managed only five uneven words: "Where do you come from?"

✳ ✳ ✳

When I was in college, I used to go to Boston on the weekends with friends. On one of our first trips during my freshman year, we noticed a peculiar man standing by the steps outside of Quincy Market. He was a bit disheveled, and he was shouting and ringing a bell. He held a homemade sign that read, "REPENT, FOR THE KINGDOM OF GOD IS AT HAND!" My friends and I were intrigued, so we asked him what his message was all about.

He must not have received many inquiries, and I think our eagerness to hear what he had to say tipped him off. He immediately asked if we were already Christians. We told him we were and he went back to ringing his bell. "God's judgment is coming," he said. "We've got to get as many people saved as possible." Then he began shouting again: "Repent! The end is near!"

After that, I never forgot this strange guy. For all four years of college and for some time after, whenever I went into Boston, I would see this man standing on a street corner, near a subway terminal, or in Boston Common. His message was always the same: *Repent or God's kingdom will get you!*

Based on what is recorded in the four Gospels, Jesus talked about one topic more than any other. You might think the number-one subject was love or forgiveness. Or perhaps you've heard that Jesus talked about hell more than He talked about heaven. You may even have read somewhere that Jesus discussed money quite a bit. All of these topics were important to Jesus, but one encompassed and outweighed them all: the kingdom of God. In some places, it's called the *kingdom of heaven,* and, in some contexts, Jesus referred to the kingdom simply as *eternal life.* Regardless of the designation, though, a person cannot read the Gospels without being struck by the fact that Jesus spent most of His time talking about an alternate reality.

The kingdom of God isn't a place; it can't be found on any map. Throughout history, nations and empires have attempted to identify themselves with God's kingdom. Sometimes there's no mistaking the identification. For instance, during the medieval period, the term *Christendom* was applied to those parts of the world where Christianity was the state religion. And it's still popular to co-opt God's kingdom for political gain in our own day. In popular culture, the United States of America is sometimes referred to as "God's country" or "the new Promised Land." America's political leaders often invoke biblical imagery in an attempt to persuade their constituencies that God has chosen to favor America above all other nations. John F. Kennedy and Ronald Reagan both famously referred to America as a shining "city on a hill," an echo of what had been written about the New World in the Mayflower Compact, and an allusion to Matthew 5:14.

But the kingdom of God is not an earthly, political domain. It's a secret kingdom that cannot be seen with natural eyes. It is an upside-down empire, where the ethics and attitudes of this world are undone. It is an ever-expanding realm without borders, and it grows wherever the sovereignty of God is heeded. It is a kingdom that began during Jesus' ministry and exists yet today, but will not be fully realized or experienced until Jesus returns. In this kingdom, there is no poverty, no hunger, and no thirst. There is no death, and there is no mourning. Debts have been forgiven and prisoners have been set free. The divisions of race, class, nationality, and denomination are meaningless. Above all, perfect harmony exists between God and His people.

This is the kingdom Jesus came to proclaim. While He traveled, He healed the sick and the lame, because in His kingdom, there is only health and wholeness. He cast out demons because Satan's darkness has no dominion in the kingdom of light. He raised the dead to let the world know that death is not the final answer in God's sovereign order. This radical, upside-down, unseen, glorious kingdom was the kingdom Jesus referred to in His short interlude with Pilate.

The kingdom of God is not something to be feared the way that street-corner preacher in Boston declared. The kingdom of God is not coming through a political leader or a particular nation. It's a kingdom that is indeed invading our planet, but it does not come with the weapons that the empires of this world use to wage war.

Though I don't know where or when, at some point, Jesus had changed Mary's life. Though she was poor, old, and hungry there in Jamaica, she was given a sneak peek at true reality and she never looked back. Faced with the pressures and realities of this present order, she chose to embrace the supernatural, glorious kingdom ushered in by Jesus.

The Bible doesn't tell us exactly what Pilate understood concerning Jesus, but the Gospel writers make it clear that it was not Pilate's idea to put him to death. In Matthew's Gospel, we read that Pilate symbolically washed his hands in front of the crowds while declaring, "I am innocent of this man's blood" (Matthew 27:24). Nevertheless, though the Jewish leaders instigated the plot to kill Jesus, it was the Roman governor who finally ordered Jesus' crucifixion.

While guards made the preparations necessary to carry out Pilate's orders, there was a peculiar exchange between Pilate and the chief priests. Pilate ordered a sign to be placed above Jesus on His cross. It read simply "Jesus of Nazareth: King of the Jews," and it was written in three languages: Greek, Aramaic, and Latin. Greek was the common trade language of the Roman Empire; Aramaic was the language of the Jewish people who lived in Judea; and Latin was the official language of Rome. Evidently, Pilate wanted this sign to be understood by *anyone* who witnessed the event.

The chief priests strenuously objected to the sign and requested it be replaced with one declaring that Jesus only *claimed to be* the king of the Jews. But Pilate would no longer acquiesce to the Jewish leaders. "What I have written, I have written" (John 19:22), he stated resolutely. He couldn't let go of the small glimpse of reality he had received from Jesus. Tragically, he could not bring himself to fully embrace it, either.

When I read the account of Jesus' interaction with Pontius Pilate, I can't help but feel sorry for Pilate. I know that may sound strange. After all, it was Jesus who was put to death, not Pilate. Still, I feel bad for the governor because he came so close, but missed out on the joy of God's kingdom. He undoubtedly perceived something special about Jesus and, as a result, made it clear that he wanted no part in Jesus' death. It seems that he understood that Jesus wasn't lying about who He said He was, but there was something that took hold of Pilate—something that he couldn't overcome—something strong enough to keep him from embracing Truth.

Perhaps the truth was simply too costly. Defending Jesus probably would have cost Pilate any ability to maintain what fragile peace existed in that perpetually tumultuous province of Judea. After all, the crowds who had gathered outside of Pilate's home were crying for blood. It might also have cost Pilate his position as governor. Would Caesar really have understood why Pilate allowed riots and bloodshed—most definitely bad for business, as well as Rome's reputation for maintaining security and the fabled *Pax Romana*—for the sake of one man, some nondescript peasant, clearly a troublemaker?

Pilate made what he thought to be a prudent decision. He chose the path of least resistance, but it cost him more than he could have possibly realized. He missed out on eternal life, the joy of knowing God, true peace and security, and the friendship of Jesus. Compared with such things, a mid-level position in the Roman government is nothing.

When I visited Jamaica, I came face to face with people who had already begun living in a new reality. It shook me to my core. What I had previously taken for granted was challenged. I saw in Mary and in the others we met something more real than anything I'd ever seen before. The experience caused me to reconsider my priorities. I went back through the Gospels and reread some of the things Jesus had said about the kingdom of God. I had a choice to make about how I would live—about how I would relate to this new understanding of reality. That's what happens when we're confronted with Jesus. We have to decide just what we'll do with Him. We must make a daily choice about how we will live in the light of this amazing truth.

When someone treats us with contempt, do we respond with what we think that person might deserve or do we respond with love? When we're confronted with poverty on the street near our home or with poverty in Uganda, do we ignore the cries we hear or do we attempt to bring to earth a short preview of the kingdom that has no hunger by providing food for those in need? When we're faced with an uncertain future, do we panic and hoard or do we rest in the security of knowing that God is truly sovereign and in control of all things? When we're faced with death, do we fear or do we recognize that there is life after death and a future resurrection and reward? This is the great challenge of the Christian life: living like strangers and aliens in a world we once thought of as home.

✶ ✶ ✶

*"He told them another parable: 'The kingdom of heaven is like a mustard seed, which a man took and planted in his field. Though it is the smallest of all seeds, yet when it grows, it is the largest of garden plants and becomes a tree, so that the birds come and perch in its branches.'" (Matthew 13:31-32)*

**Chapter Eight: The Most Important Question Ever Asked**
**Questions for Reflection & Discussion:**

1) Do you believe the kingdom of God is a present or a future reality? Or do you believe it is both? Why?

2) There is a famous quotation, often attributed to Francis of Assisi: "Preach the gospel at all times and when necessary use words." What do you think of this statement in light of this chapter's discussion of the kingdom of God?

3) The Romans believed that the secret to life could be found in strength and military power, while many of the Jewish people of the first century believed the key to a blessed life was obedience to religious rules and regulations. What are some of the modern versions of reality competing with the truth of the kingdom today?

CHAPTER NINE

# The Vertical Deathbed Confession

All You Need Is Faith

✲ ✲ ✲

## Luke 23:32-43
## The Thieves Crucified with Jesus

✲ ✲ ✲

**SUGGESTED LISTENING**

Travis Oberg, "Hurricane," from *Bloodlines*

J. J. Heller: "Save Me," from *Painted Red*

# The Vertical Deathbed Confession
## All You Need Is Faith

*Today has been a terrible day*, he thought, *the worst day of my life.* The absolute truth of this fact had been painfully pounded into his awareness via the iron nails that impaled his hands and feet. Sure, there had been other pain-filled days in the past. He thought about the nights when he went hungry. He remembered being isolated and alone, when everyone he cared about had left him. He thought about prison, and his body recalled what it felt like to be beaten unconscious. But this—being nailed to a cross and left for dead—was the worst pain he had ever experienced. He had already lost a lot of blood and the sun had dehydrated him. But the worst part was that he couldn't breathe. A short time before, just after he had been nailed in place, the soldiers lifted the cross up vertically; then they dropped it into a hole in the ground to secure it. The impact of the cross falling into that hole had dislocated his shoulders, making it impossible to lift himself up with his upper body to get a breath. He was reduced to pushing himself up with his legs to breathe. The pain from the nails in his feet and hands was unbearable. Add to all this pain the realization that this would be his last day on earth, and yes, this was the worst day of his life.

Through the sweat in his eyes, the criminal could see a large crowd coming up the road. At the front of the rabble, another prisoner was being brought out to Golgotha to be crucified. Though He was still a considerable distance away, it looked like the man was even weaker than he'd been. He collapsed every few feet and the soldiers kicked him every time He fell. After a while, the soldiers, frustrated with the delay, yanked a dark-skinned man from the crowd and gruffly ordered him to carry the cross for the now half-dead prisoner.

"He must have done something even worse than us," another prisoner said, hanging on a cross just a few yards away—no longer his partner in crime, now they would be partners in death. As the new prisoner drew closer, they could see He'd been beaten badly. Blood covered His face, arms, and legs. His back was one large, open sore. The throng of people following this man was far larger than one would expect for the crucifixion of most criminals. The two men on crosses looked at each other with an unspoken understanding. The people of Jerusalem were so vehement, so incensed; this man must have done something truly abominable.

As the soldiers nailed the man to his cross, the two criminals noticed the sign placed above His head on the vertical wooden beam. It read: "Jesus of Nazareth: King of the Jews." *Jesus of Nazareth?* They'd heard of this man. He was a teacher, a miracle-worker, and a prophet—or at least, such was the rumor—but they had not heard a thing about Him engaging in any illegal activity; He was no criminal. They had only heard that this Jesus had helped people, healed them of diseases, and set them free from evil spirits. *What could he have done to wind up here with us?* one of the young men thought. The other, more cynical, thought, *I knew it. He was just a con-artist—a criminal like us.*

As they raised Jesus up, the two men hanging beside Him could see the anguish on his face. They understood it better than anyone else. Still, the people milling about just below were not satisfied. They mocked Jesus and hurled insults. Hours earlier, when the two criminals had been nailed to their crosses, they had fought their fate, kicking and screaming with every ounce of strength they possessed. They had cursed and shouted in anger at the people who had come to watch them die. But this man was different. At first, they thought that perhaps He was just too tired to fight back or shout at the crowds. But then, they heard Jesus say something: "Father, forgive them, for they do not know what they are doing" (Luke 23:34). It wasn't shouted, but it was said clearly enough for all to hear, and it was evident that this request was directed toward heaven.

The two men hanging next to Jesus—one on his right and one on his left—saw the same scene and the same Jesus. Yet, their responses to Him couldn't have been more different. The Gospel of Luke tells us that one of the thieves added to the mockery, yelling to Jesus, "Aren't you the Messiah? Save yourself and us!" (Luke 23:39). He couldn't believe in Jesus because he saw the blood and the apparent weakness Jesus displayed. The other man, however, saw something different. He defended Jesus, telling the other criminal, "Don't you fear God... since you are under the same sentence? We are punished justly, for we are getting what our deeds deserve. But this man has done nothing wrong" (Luke 23:40-41). Instead of weakness, he saw power, beauty, and authenticity.

Both men were facing death, but one man looked at the world he was soon to leave and the man who claimed to be the Deliverer and Savior and responded with anger. I know he's the *bad guy* in this story, but I can understand where he's coming from. No matter what I had done wrong, I think it would be hard not to be angry, hanging there naked, nailed to a Roman cross. And I can't really blame him for not getting it. A bloodied, half-dead carpenter is not exactly what one calls to mind when one considers what the Son of God might look like. I'd like to think that I would be like the other criminal—the *good one* who recognized that Jesus was special—but, if I'm honest, I have to admit that I judge with my eyes more often than not.

The *good criminal* (for lack of a better descriptor) saw something special in Jesus. Maybe he had heard stories about the carpenter. Maybe it was the way Jesus didn't fight the soldiers or curse the crowds. Perhaps it could have been that Jesus prayed for the forgiveness of those who were, at that very moment, killing Him. Something made him take Jesus' side. Something yanked this man out of his own very natural, very human perspective and shifted him to a place where he could adopt Jesus' viewpoint. Something made him ask Jesus for a first and final favor, though it was a struggle even to breathe, let alone talk: "Jesus, remember me when you come into your kingdom" (Luke 23:42). Whatever it was, his faith in the newfound Messiah was remarkable.

✡ ✡ ✡

In 1942, Father William Cummings gave a stirring sermon in the fields of Bataan, in which he made the now-famous statement, "There are no atheists in foxholes." The idea is that, when we're faced with our own mortality, every human being seems compelled to believe in God—if only so that He might be sought for immediate protection. People who, under normal circumstances, would scoff at the idea of heaven or of needing Jesus as a Savior suddenly find faith when they've no place else to turn. Some might argue that the good criminal on the cross was a foxhole believer. He had nothing left to lose; he was most assuredly going to die. So hey, why not give Jesus a nod, just in case there was something to this Messiah business? I think it's safe to say that this criminal did have nothing left to lose, but that doesn't necessarily mean his faith was disingenuous. Jesus' favorable response tells us that it was the real thing: "Truly I tell you, today you will be with me in paradise" (Luke 23:43).

I think God sometimes allows us to go (or takes us) to a place where we have nothing to lose, so that in our desperation, we might cry out to Him. If we consider our desperate circumstance in that light, then the act of God bringing us to the very end of ourselves—whether such circumstance comes from something we've done or something outside of our control—is sweet grace in action. We don't have to be facing certain death to experience this kind of grace, either. This outpouring of God's compassion can come when we're alone, when we're scared, or when we don't know which way to turn in a mixed-up, confused time of life. God wants us to know that we're not really alone, we've no reason to be afraid, and that we can always turn to Him.

✳ ✳ ✳

*What must I do to be saved?* In one form or another, that's a question that was asked quite often during Jesus' ministry, and it's a question that still gets asked a lot today. We toss around the idea that there's nothing *we* can do—that it's all faith and grace—but that seems too easy. We think life and death is like a road-trip to Canada. It would be horrible to drive for hours and then get to the border and find out you're missing your passport. So it is with heaven. We want something we can hold in our hands, something we can see, to make sure we'll get across that border. We want a checklist or a seven or ten or twelve-step solution to follow—something that will give us credentials to get past those pearly gates. We want to be sure we've checked whatever boxes must be checked before it's too late.

I never really knew my grandfather on my mother's side. As far as I can remember, I've only met him a handful of times. He married my grandmother in 1952, but to my grandmother's shock, it turned out that their marriage was invalid because he was already married. My grandfather had another wife and other children, another house, and another life. When my mother and my uncle were young, their father would pop in and out of their lives from time to time, but for the most part, they grew up without ever really getting to know him. And it wasn't until I was a teenager that my mother's father tried to make contact with her again.

My mother's stepfather was the grandpa I grew up with, and I wasn't interested in getting to know someone else, especially someone who had abandoned and hurt my grandmother, my mother, and my uncle. When he did get in touch with her, my mom was generally excited to reconnect with her long-lost father, but I couldn't understand her eagerness, and I was somewhat wary. My grandmother (my mother's mother) had died many years earlier, so I couldn't exactly get her side of the story. All I had were the reports passed down from relatives about how things had happened. I decided it didn't matter though. I just couldn't trust someone who could walk out on his family—even if he had two of them. I also thought that being nice to this newfound biological grandfather would be a slap in the face to the man who had been a real grandfather to me my whole life. Still, I was just a bit curious; there were some things I might learn.[27]

When we walked into the restaurant where my family had agreed to meet our lost patriarch, I didn't know what to expect. He had arrived first and was waiting to greet us with a big smile and hugs. It was an odd sight. He was a gray-haired man in his late sixties, but he looked like me—or I looked like him, I suppose.[28] What was most surprising, however, was that he wasn't a jerk. He was charming, confident, funny, good-looking, and generally nice to be around. He even smelled good. It was no wonder my grandmother had fallen for him.

After lunch, we drove to my grandfather's house to continue our visit. Before we left, he asked if my sister, brother, and I would like to ride with him in his car. I still wasn't sure how to process all of this. I mean, can you really just gloss over decades of neglect? What happened all those years ago was still affecting our family. But here was this charming, handsome, in-charge guy who looked just like me, and who wanted to get to know me. I took the ride.

Before we got to his house, though, my new grandfather made a stop we hadn't expected. He pulled up to a church that was old, gray, and worn. It had the spires and architectural details that let you know that the building, though it was probably less than a hundred years old, was part of something ancient and holy. It was a Roman Catholic church, and he had stopped to say a prayer for my grandmother. Now, as I mentioned previously, my grandmother had died years earlier, so I didn't quite get what we were doing. Walking into the church,

---

27 They say male pattern baldness is hereditary, passed down through your mother's genes. This would be my opportunity to find out if I might be bald someday.

28 To my relief, he still had a mostly-full head of hair.

my grandfather knelt down in a pew toward the back of the sanctuary and made the sign of the cross. My sister and I looked at one another. We kneeled as well, though we flubbed the sign. My little brother just watched. Then, making his way to the very back of the church, this man that we knew nothing about did something odd. He pulled some quarters out of his pocket and fed them into a slot near some candles that were behind glass. Suddenly, four of the candles lit themselves.

Back in the car, he explained that lighting the candles would alert a nun serving at the church to say a prayer for our grandmother. He also explained that it was wrong for my mother to leave the Catholic church, and that we needed to return to it or risk making God angry. He also told us that our grandmother was probably in purgatory, and that's why we needed to pray for her. This was all very foreign and odd to me. Praying for the dead? Purgatory? Coin-operated prayer candles? Just who was this strange guy we had heard about all of our lives, but hadn't met until just today?

After this first visit, we saw my grandfather a few more times, but then with less frequency. He would send us cards and notes from time to time, some with a picture of a monastery or an abbey. There would be a note indicating that a donation was made in our names, so that the brothers or sisters of a particular order would pray for our souls. My grandfather would also send us money now and then. It was hard to complain about getting money in the mail, but it soon became obvious that the cards and cash didn't have much to do with us. And even his decision to contact us after so many years wasn't really about us.

These things were all about him; the god he worshipped demanded penance. He needed to try and make up for what he had done wrong or else, as he believed was true of my grandmother, he'd end up in purgatory for a long period of time, paying for his sins through suffering. The god to whom my grandfather paid homage is not the God of the Bible.

Please don't misunderstand me. Above all else, what matters most is not our denominational affiliation or our religious tradition; it's what we do with Jesus and what He's done on our behalf. The true God of the Bible doesn't require that we earn our way to heaven or that we suffer for our sins if we've honestly confessed those sins to Him, asked for His forgiveness, turned away from those sins, and turned to Him in faith.[29] That's what the cross is all about. Jesus paid the price for our sins, so we don't have to. After all, no matter how much we suffered, no matter how many repetitious or lengthy prayers we recited, no matter how many good deeds we did, we would never be able to make up for sins committed against an infinitely holy God. That's why we need grace.[30] That's why all that's required to be saved is that we believe. But don't make the mistake of thinking that that word *believe* is the cheap thing we often mean today when we use the term. The word *believe,* as used in the Bible, means "to trust in, rely on, depend on, and obey." It's a lot more than simply *believing* something in your head.

Jesus was crucified between two thieves. Both were guilty and were receiving the earthly consequences for their actions. One of these men turned to Jesus and taunted Him, shouting for Jesus to save Himself and His fellow prisoners. This criminal couldn't see past this world; he couldn't see that a more important judgment awaited him. The other thief, however,

29 By the way, if the whole idea of *faith* is still a bit fuzzy, let me try to explain what Christians mean when they use that term. *Turning to Jesus in faith* is what a person does when they *turn away* from living life the way they were living—they stop submitting to the sins of their past, and instead submit to Jesus' rule in their lives. They *turn to* Jesus in obedience as He talks to them and gives them direction and guidance each day.
30 *Grace* has been defined as "unmerited or undeserved favor," or as the saying goes, "getting what you don't deserve."

recognized that he would soon be standing before God with nothing of his own to offer in his defense. Somehow, hanging on that cross next to Jesus, this hardened criminal was softened. Turning to the man he now understood to be the true King, he asked for a pardon. He trusted in, depended upon, and relied on Jesus because he didn't have *anything else* upon which to rely at that point in his life. And Jesus, recognizing the man's complete dependency upon Him, his complete surrender to Him, and his complete trust in Him, granted him release. When you think about it, a few hours of pain served to bring this man to the end of himself. There he had nothing else upon which he could depend; nothing else in which he could trust; and nothing else on which he could rely. But it was there that he found Jesus, and it was there that he received eternal life. What an incredible bargain.

When the Roman soldiers came around to clean up the site, the Gospel writers tell us that they broke the legs of the two men who were crucified on either side of Jesus.[31] Breaking the legs prohibited a crucifixion victim from pushing themselves up to take a breath. As a result, death came much more quickly through suffocation. However, this was not common practice. Depending on the condition of the person prior to being nailed to the cross, it could take up to several days for a victim to succumb to death (this is one of the elements of crucifixion that made it so horrific), and the Romans were not normally in a rush to hasten their executions. The more suffering and anguish these criminals experienced, the more the people who viewed these scenes would fear the power of the empire. In this case, however, the Romans made an exception. They did this because

---

31 It was not necessary to break Jesus' legs, because He was already dead before the Roman soldiers got to Him. Instead, just to make sure He was truly dead, one of the soldiers pierced His side. John tells us that blood and water poured from Jesus' wound. See John 19:33-35.

the Jewish leaders had asked that the bodies be removed before the next day's special Passover Sabbath celebration.

To these soldiers and to any onlookers, these two criminals suffered the same fate, with nothing to distinguish one from the other. But appearances aren't everything. One of these men had scoffed at Jesus and the idea of faith; he was lost forever. The other man, just as guilty of the same crimes on earth, was welcomed into Paradise alongside the Carpenter-King he had met so briefly that day. The last and worst day of this criminal's earthly life turned out to be the first day of a beautiful, glorious, and pain-free life that will never end.

I think this account of the thief on the cross was included in the New Testament because it reminds us that anything we do, no matter how noble or sacrificial, in an attempt to earn our way into His favor is, in God's eyes, just garbage. There are other passages in the Bible that convey this truth, of course, but this account is a living picture of grace in action. This criminal, exposed and hanging just meters from Jesus, couldn't have brought anything to the Lord if he tried. He had no possessions to offer, no good works he could do. Crucifixion was reserved for the vilest of offenders, and though Scripture doesn't tell us exactly what his crimes were, we can be confident that they weren't light misdemeanors. The only thing he could bring to Jesus was his faith—his utter dependence, surrender, reliance, and trust. And that's all we can bring Him too, no matter who we are or what we've done; it's the only thing He accepts. And that is the best of news.

✽ ✽ ✽

*"For it is by grace you have been saved, through faith—and this is not from yourselves, it is the gift of God—not by works, so that no one can boast." (Ephesians 2:8-9)*

**Chapter Nine: The Vertical Deathbed Confession**
**Questions for Reflection & Discussion:**

1) Do you agree with the author's statement, "I think God sometimes allows us to go (or takes us) to a place where we have nothing to lose, so that in our desperation, we might cry out to Him. If we consider our desperate circumstance in that light, then the act of God bringing us to the very end of ourselves—whether such circumstance comes from something we've done or something outside of our control—is sweet grace in action." Why or why not?

2) Take a few minutes to reflect on your own life and on God's grace. Can you remember a time when you lived as though God's favor was something that could be earned?

3) Does it make you uncomfortable that God's grace cannot be earned? Why or why not?

CHAPTER TEN

# Not By Sight

The Blessing of Missing It

✡ ✡ ✡

## John 20:24-29
## Thomas

✡ ✡ ✡

**SUGGESTED LISTENING**

Andrew Peterson: "The Good Confession (I Believe),"
from *Resurrection Letters, Volume II*

Jake Armerding: "Adonai," from *Jake Armerding*

# Not By Sight
## The Blessing of Missing It

Thomas wasn't there with Mary at the tomb. He wasn't with the other disciples when Jesus appeared to them either. It seemed that everyone close to Jesus had seen Him since He was raised from the dead—everyone except Thomas. And Thomas wasn't sure what to believe. He'd heard the stories and he trusted his friends, but this just sounded so bizarre, so out there. He thought about it constantly. It just didn't make sense. *If God had planned to raise Jesus from the dead all along, why did He let Him die in the first place?*

Thomas wanted to believe; he really did. It was just that he had already been disappointed so badly. He had hoped that Jesus was going to put things right. He had believed Jesus was the Messiah God had promised, and like most of the Jews of his generation, he'd been taught that when the Messiah came, He'd establish the Jews in their own land and free them from oppression. He had so desperately wanted Jesus to be the One who would finally bring peace and justice and rest.

But then he watched as soldiers came and took Jesus away. He heard about how Jesus was brought before Pilate, and how

He barely uttered a word in His own defense. Thomas couldn't bear to witness the crucifixion, but the news was all over Jerusalem. The One in whom he had put all his trust and hope did what seemed impossible just days before—*He died*. The man who had healed people of leprosy, who had calmed the storm, who had walked on water, who had raised the dead, had Himself succumbed to death.

After all of this, Thomas vowed never to let himself hope again. He wouldn't believe anything unless he saw it with his own two eyes. That's why, when his friends came to him and told him that they had seen Jesus alive, he could only say, "Unless I see the nail marks in his hands and put my finger where the nails were, and put my hand into his side, I will not believe" (John 20:25). As far as Thomas was concerned, the time for faith[32] had passed. He had already paid that price and had been severely disillusioned.

For about a week, Thomas was convinced he'd made the right decision. While the other disciples were running around sharing sensational stories and acting like madmen, he had retained his dignity. He hadn't quite gotten back to life's normal routine, and there was still a part of him that carelessly wanted to believe, but he knew that keeping his resolve was the only way to avoid the pain he had experienced when Jesus was taken away.

And then, one evening when he was with the other disciples, he heard a familiar voice from behind. "Peace be with you!" (John 20:26). Turning quickly, Thomas' eyes fixed upon the most beautiful thing he'd ever seen. There He was—Jesus Himself—standing right in front of him. But how could this be? The door was locked. No one had knocked on it, and no one had opened it. *A ghost perhaps*, Thomas thought. Even with the

---

32 Hebrews 11:1 defines *faith* as "being sure of what we hope for and certain of what we do not see."

Lord apparently just a few feet away from him, he didn't want to make even the smallest leap of faith. Jesus looked at him. "See My hands. Touch where the nails were," He said. "And look at My side; place your hand where I was pierced." At that moment, a wave of release came over Thomas; he could believe again. All the hidden doubts crumbled into oblivion, and he was free.

✲ ✲ ✲

I remember sitting in Bible class in junior high school. I can recall watching a movie about Noah's ark. It wasn't a cheesy, made-for-TV effort though; it was a documentary. There was this guy who claimed to have seen Noah's boat, still mostly intact, atop an isolated mountain in Turkey. He even had a photograph taken from an airplane as evidence. The photo was out of focus and the alleged ark was in the distance—really small. You had to have someone point it out to you, but if you looked just right, you could sort of see this dark, rectangular outline of a boat... or at least it could have been a boat. It was quite fuzzy.

That same video had an interview with another man who claimed to have an actual piece of Noah's ark: a chunk of petrified wood he believed could be dated back to the supposed time of the flood. He said he had found the block of wood in the same area of Turkey that the picture of the ark had been taken. The piece of wood looked more like a rock, though. I guessed that's what they meant by "petrified."

Still, as a seventh-grader, the video was quite convincing. They had found Noah's ark! How could anyone doubt the story now? Sure, on its own, the story is a bit hard to swallow: This really old guy builds a giant boat and then collects two of every animal because God told him He was going to destroy the entire world with a flood. So, without even raising his hand to ask a question, he builds this boat in his backyard as the neighbors laugh at him. And then it rains for forty days and forty nights and everything that lived on the earth (including those neighbors) is wiped out—everything except Noah's family and the creatures he'd tucked into the ark. After a long while, the waters subside, and Noah and his family start the world over again. Oh yeah, and also… that's why there are rainbows. It's no wonder this story had always been a tough sell to nonbelievers, but now there was photographic evidence and this funny-shaped piece of wood (which really looked more like a rock) to prove it. Bible—1, bad guys—0.

A few weeks later, we had an exam in that Bible class. One of the questions read something like, "How do we know that the story of Noah's ark really happened?" I was ready for this one. I cracked my knuckles and began to write. I explained about the photographs and the different eyewitnesses to the discovery of ancient wooden beams. I wrote line upon line about how strange it was that wood, which had been shaped with tools, had been found on the top of a mountain, and how one man actually brought back a small piece. I ran out of space, so I turned the page over and continued. I mentioned that we probably would have already recovered the ark itself if it weren't for the Turkish government and a big conspiracy to keep it all a secret. When I was done, I wrapped up my answer as proficiently as I could: "In conclusion, all of this stuff proves that Noah's ark really happened."

When I got my test back, I was shocked. There was a big X next to the Noah's Ark question and a note from my Bible teacher: "Very interesting, but we know the story of Noah's ark really happened because God said it did. It's in the Bible!"

That was my first lesson in hard faith.[33] There's no point waiting until some scientist or celebrity or philosopher makes an airtight case as though they've proven what God has already declared. That's just not going to happen, at least not the way we want it to. Yes, there is great value in biblical archaeology, and it is exciting to know that many discoveries have affirmed precisely what the Bible tells us. Still, no amount of biblical archaeology or other evidence is ever going to *prove* the Bible. There's never going to come a day when the world's scientists and scholars announce that they've finished examining all of the evidence, and they've all come to a unanimous decision— that every word of the Bible is correct, and that every event described in it is accurate. But that's okay; there's no need for corroborating testimony from a bunch of highly respected authorities.[34] God has instead simply ordained that thing called *faith*; it's part of His plan. He decided that too much concrete evidence is not a good thing. There is more value in just taking God at his word. Faith is for our benefit.

I love my wife Melinda and I enjoy spending time with her. I know it sounds cliché, but she really is my best friend. I'd rather hang out with her than with anyone else. Life is just better when she's around. But do you know when I realize this the most? When she's *not* around. When we're separated because I need to go on a business trip or we have conflicting work schedules, I really miss being with her. Not seeing her for a time reveals what's going on in my heart in ways that spending every moment with her never could. When I get home and our schedules are in sync so we can be together, I don't care about anything else. It's all about Melinda.

---

33 I also learned a lesson about the importance of reading exams carefully to look for trick questions.

34 I'm certainly not suggesting that we should ignore scholarship; only that it's a poor substitute for faith.

It works that way with God. When we don't understand why some things happen, *that's* when we realize we need God the most. And it's when we see the true brokenness of this world that we realize we were created for another. God longs for us to turn to Him in faith, but we are too easily tripped up by miracles and signs—things so easily seen. Though such things are intended to bolster our faith, they can instead become the object of our faith. And anything that takes the place of God—even one of His miracles—is not good for us.

Jesus came into contact with this kind of misplaced faith shortly after he fed five thousand men (plus women and children) with five loaves of bread and two fish. Such a sign must have been an amazing thing to see. It's hard to imagine how anyone could miss who Jesus was after such a demonstration. Yet, when some who were there found Him later on, Jesus said to them, "Very truly I tell you, you are looking for me, not because you saw the signs I performed but because you ate the loaves and had your fill" (John 6:26). In other words, they went looking for Jesus, not because He's the Son of God and the source of eternal life (as evidenced by the amazing miracle they had just witnessed), but because He gave them something to eat. Talk about an adventure in missing the point! For these misguided folks, the signs themselves—the evidence for God and His kingdom—were all they wanted. They'd missed the most important thing: that the bread they ate was only intended to point to Jesus, who is Himself true bread—the Bread of Life. They could not see that the bread we eat is only a symbol. Just as the bread we eat nourishes, satisfies and sustains our physical bodies, Jesus nourishes, satisfies, and sustains our souls.[35]

---

35 Another example of God's people mistaking the symbol for the real thing can be found in 2 Kings 18:4. The bronze serpent that God had instructed Moses to craft (Numbers 21:4-9; see Chapter Four) as an instrument of healing had now become an object of worship—an idol that distracted the people of Israel from truly following God. It just goes to show that anything—no matter how sacred—can get in the way of true faith if we let it.

I mean, really... it's like spending a week in the car driving to Disneyland, then being so fixated on the big picture of Mickey Mouse hanging outside the gate that you never even bother to get out of the car and enter into the park.

That's what can happen to us without faith. It seems to be human nature to put other, tangible, more easily seen things in the place of God, when God Himself is the One our hearts have been searching for all along. Thomas almost missed out. He had decided that faith was too dangerous and God too mysterious. He decided he needed hard evidence, and he wasn't going to believe the reports about Jesus until he saw Him with his own two eyes and felt His wounds with his own two hands. But that kind of thinking is more dangerous than faith. Thomas almost missed out on everything that matters most, all because he was afraid to be hurt again.

I was born cross-eyed. I've been told that a lot of babies are born that way, and that their eyes naturally correct themselves shortly thereafter. Mine, however, did not; my eyes were stubborn. So, for the first several months of my life, I stared at my own nose. In addition to being cross-eyed, I also have a severe astigmatism: the view of my nose, therefore, was not only boring but also very blurry.

My parents were understandably concerned, so they took me from specialist to specialist, trying to find answers. The prognosis was grim. There was nothing the doctors could do. A few of them even speculated that I would probably go blind at some point in the near future. This was, of course, not what my parents wanted to hear, so they kept trying different doctors until they got a different answer. There was one doctor in New York City who offered to perform an experimental eye surgery that might straighten my eyes out, at least in theory. It was a long shot, but it was something.

A chance is better than no chance at all. So, at the tender age of nine months, I had surgery. My right eye was removed and then reattached. To my parents' relief, the surgery was successful. Afterwards, I still had a severe visual impairment, but it was nothing that glasses couldn't rectify. I also had to wear a patch over my left eye several hours a day for the next several years. This not only made me look like a pirate,[36] but also helped to strengthen the vision in my right eye.

Everything with my eyes went as well as could be expected until I was in the first grade. During an annual check-up, my ophthalmologist discovered that my right eye was moving back. He checked again and again, comparing images and charts, but there was no denying it—I was going cross-eyed again. I didn't know this, of course. My parents kept it from me because there was no reason to scare a little kid until they knew what had to be done. Eventually, it was determined that another eye operation was in order, but my parents still didn't tell me. I guess they were waiting until the day of the surgery, but that day never came.

The night before my scheduled operation, my mom was watching religious television—the Christian Broadcasting Network (or something like it). I was not impressed. I had no interest in watching an old, heavy-set gentleman with a Southern accent talk about the Bible. I wanted to play ColecoVision, but we only had one TV. So, as I waited for my turn to play Donkey Kong, I sat down on the floor Indian-style and listened to what the man in the bad suit had to say.

He must have been getting to the end of his talk because the camera was now really close to his face and he was a bit sweaty.

---

36 That is, if pirates wore self-adhesive patches that looked more like big band-aids than eye-patches.

He was praying with his eyes closed, pausing every few minutes to dab the moisture off of his forehead with his handkerchief. He was talking to God, but he was also talking to his viewers at home. He would say things like, "There's a woman, Lord. She's sitting at home on her couch watching this program, and she's just found out today she has cancer. Free her body of that cancer, Lord." Then, he would put God on hold and give directions to the woman at home with the cancer: "Ma'am, if you can hear my voice, stand up and walk to your television. Put your hands on the TV as a sign of faith. God is going to heal you." There were more prayers like this one. There was one for a man with a severe back problem, and another for an older woman with arthritis. He didn't call out names or the specifics of the ailment. He just gave a brief description of the health problem and a short instruction.

Then, he got to one that I thought I could try. "There's someone out there who's got a problem in their head. I don't know if it's a tumor or a headache, but there's something in your head. Something's not right, but God's going to heal you. Put your hands on your forehead. Feel God's warmth come over you. He's healing you right now." Now, I didn't have a headache or a tumor, and I didn't know that I had an eye problem that required a very serious operation. I just wanted to know if God would make my head warm like the man on the TV said He would. So I did it. I put both my hands on my forehead.

At first, there was nothing. But then, just a few short seconds later, my head felt really, really hot. It wasn't like a fever; it was more like the sensation you get from sleeping with your head under the covers. I turned around to my mom, who was falling asleep on the couch, and shouted, "Mom! I did what the man said to do, and now my head is hot!"

My mom was initially confused. "What do you mean it's 'hot'? Are you feeling okay?" I explained what the man on TV had said, and how he told me to put my hands on my head, and how God had healed me—of what, I was not sure, of course. I just knew that the preacher said my head would get hot, and so it had!

The next morning, my parents expected that I would have surgery. They drove me to the hospital, though they still hadn't told me what was going on. I thought I was just going for another doctor's visit. I don't know if my mom was holding out hope that I really had been healed, or if my parents were just waiting until the last possible moment to tell me that I was going to have surgery. It didn't matter though, because as the doctor conducted one more routine check of my eyes, he noticed something very strange. He checked again and again, but he finally confirmed it: My right eye had straightened out on its own. In just the few short weeks since my last visit, when it was determined that I would need the operation, my eye had miraculously gone back to normal.

I didn't share the story about my eye being healed to prove to you that miracles happen. I believe they do, but telling you the story doesn't prove it. Even if you trust me and believe I wouldn't purposely lead you astray, my testimony is still just that—one person's testimony. It's not concrete proof. The events in the story did happen. I remember watching the preacher on TV and I remember my head burning. My mom even called the show to tell them what had happened, and the next night, the host of the show mentioned me on the air. None of that, however, can ever prove to you that I was healed.

I don't share that story too often. This is partly because it happened so long ago, and it's hard to discern between memories of the events themselves and the impressions I got from hearing the story so many times as a kid. But I also don't share it too often because I think it can be pretty hard to swallow. I have told close friends and other people when appropriate. Amazingly, I've never had anyone tell me that they didn't believe me. I have had people ask me why God didn't finish the job and heal my eyes entirely so I wouldn't need glasses or contacts. I tell them I don't know why that is, but I'll make sure to ask Him someday.

I don't know why God hasn't given me perfect vision, but my guess is that it's the same reason He doesn't give us perfect spiritual vision. What I mean is this: We all see in part. The Bible says that "we see only a reflection as in a mirror" (1 Corinthians 13:12). We can almost, but not quite perfectly, discern what's going on if we pay close attention, but we're never going to receive a clear, full picture of God or His plans this side of eternity. What we can observe will only take us so far; the rest is up to faith. And that's what keeps us dependent on God.

At first glance, this might imply that God is mean. Seriously, what kind of loving God would purposely keep His children at a disadvantage just so they remain dependent upon Him? When people do this sort of thing, it's ugly and dysfunctional. But when God does it, it's actually the most loving thing He can do. God is the only one upon whom we should depend. We ought to trust Him and look to Him all the time, for while in people we are always eventually disappointed, when we place our trust and dependence upon Him, we *never* are.[37]

---

[37] I don't intend to minimize the experiences of people who depend on God but who are still met with disappointment in life. What I mean is that God Himself is never the source of our disappointment.

Even if we were capable of figuring everything out and taking care of ourselves, that still wouldn't be a good thing. We aren't perfect. Every one of us makes mistakes, and the Bible says that we're all corrupted by sin. That means that if we only depend on ourselves or even on each other, we're going to miss the mark. We're just not going to get things right.

God wants us to live in relationship with Him. He wants to walk through this life with us. He wants our stories to become part of His story. It's the reason we were created, it brings glory to God, and it's the best thing possible for us.

Thomas is sometimes called "doubting Thomas," but to be fair, any of the disciples would have done the same, had they missed seeing the resurrected Jesus. I'm sure that Thomas wondered why, at first, Jesus had appeared to the other disciples when he wasn't around. The others didn't really have any more faith than he did. They had just gotten to see Jesus before Thomas. For us who live today, we find ourselves in the same position. We missed Jesus' first appearance, and we're still waiting for Him to return.

It's like the old hymn, "It Is Well with My Soul," written by Horatio Spafford. Mr. Spafford knew something about faith. During the great Chicago fire of 1871, his only son perished. On top of that, the damage from the fire ruined him financially. Stricken with grief, he and his wife planned to relocate to Europe and start over. Horatio needed to remain behind in Chicago to tie up some loose ends, so he sent his wife and four daughters ahead. Then the unthinkable happened. A telegram arrived from Europe; it contained only two words: "Saved alone." The ship that carried his wife and daughters across the Atlantic had collided with another vessel and sank. The telegram was notification that only Horatio's wife had survived. Spafford traveled to meet his wife in Europe, and as his ship passed over the spot where his daughters had died, he wrote these words:

*"And Lord, haste the day when my faith shall be sight,*
*The clouds be rolled back as a scroll;*
*The trump shall resound, and the Lord shall descend,*
*Even so, it is well with my soul."*

For Horatio Spafford, there were no easy answers; only questions. The refrain of this hymn is telling. Even with all he had lost, he had faith, and he could still say, "It is well with my soul." His troubled mind could find rest, not because he had everything figured out to his satisfaction, but because he had Jesus. As Spafford penned, there will come a day when faith is no longer required, when the veil between the natural and the supernatural is torn and our questions are answered. But, until that day, our vision is fuzzy. The gospel is good news, but it's good news that must be received by faith, and not by sight. Such a dynamic is for our benefit. Jesus was talking about you and me when he said to Thomas, "Because you have seen me, you have believed; *blessed are those who have not seen and yet have believed*" (John 20:29; italics added).

*"For in the gospel the righteousness of God is revealed—a righteousness that is by faith from first to last, just as it is written: 'The righteous will live by faith.'" (Romans 1:17)*

**Chapter Ten: Not By Sight**
**Questions for Reflection & Discussion:**

1) Do you have trouble believing in miracles? If so, why do you think that is?

2) Do you agree with the author's statement that "faith is for our benefit"? Why or why not?

3) If you are a Christian, when was the last time you were in a situation that required faith? If it's been a while, ask God to show you opportunities to depend upon Him. He may put it on your heart to talk with someone at school or work about Jesus, or He may ask you to give sacrificially to someone in need this month. Whatever it is, use the situation as a means of growing in your faith.

# God Recycles

## Everything Has a Redemption Value

✠ ✠ ✠

---

# Acts 9:1-6
# Paul

---

✠ ✠ ✠

**SUGGESTED LISTENING**

Sixpence None the Richer: "The Ground You Shook," from *Greatest Hits*

Jars of Clay, "Trouble Is," from *Who We Are Instead*

---

38 To paraphrase Christopher Guest from *This is Spinal Tap*, "What do you do when you're on Chapter Ten and you need that extra push over the cliff? Where can you go from there? Normally, nowhere. Except this book goes to Chapter Eleven!"

# God Recycles
## Everything Has a Redemption Value

On the song, *Fly from Heaven*, Glen Phillips of Toad the Wet Sprocket, sings these words about the apostle Paul:

*"Paul is making me nervous;*
*Paul is making me scared.*
*Into this room, he swaggers*
*Like he's God's own messenger."*[39]

*God's own messenger?* That's quite a statement, but there is a sense in which, more than any of the other New Testament writers, Paul really was God's messenger. With more books of the Bible attributed to him than to anyone else, God gave Paul a lot to say.

It was Paul who wrote the famous passage on love found in the thirteenth chapter of his first letter to the Corinthian church (the same passage you've probably heard recited at more than one wedding), and it was Paul who so succinctly

---

39 Toad the Wet Sprocket, "Fly from Heaven," *Dulcinea,* © 1994 Sony Music Entertainment Inc.

summed up the concept of grace with these words: "For the wages of sin is death, but the gift of God is eternal life in Christ Jesus our Lord" (Romans 6:23). Paul's writings informed St. Augustine's theological framework, and they inspired Martin Luther's conceptual understanding of *justification by faith alone.* Samuel Coleridge called Paul's letter to the Roman church "the most profound work in existence." Generations of believers, facing tremendous uncertainty and persecution, have been encouraged by these words from Paul: "For I am convinced that neither death nor life, neither angels nor demons, neither the present nor the future, nor any powers, neither height nor depth, nor anything else in all creation, will be able to separate us from the love of God that is in Christ Jesus our Lord" (Romans 8:38-39).

Paul was also a church planter. He established many of the early churches we read about in the New Testament, and his missionary journeys were one of the vehicles through which the gospel extended across the ancient world of the first century.

He was even a civil rights leader. When the Church began, it was comprised solely of Jewish believers, but Paul considered himself the apostle to the Gentiles (anyone who is not ethnically Jewish), and brought the good news to places where people did not know the God who revealed Himself in the Old Testament. He understood that God's desire is for *one* holy people, with no wall of separation between Jews and Gentiles. He was so convicted that the truth of the gospel demanded an end to prejudice that, on one occasion, he publicly rebuked the apostle Peter (someone who had been with Jesus from the early days of His ministry) for refusing to eat a meal with his Gentile brothers in Christ (see Galatians 2:11-13).

Unquestionably, the apostle Paul has been one of God's most effective tools in establishing, growing, and reforming the Church. But you would not have expected such a thing as you read through the Gospels. Paul is mentioned nowhere in Matthew, Mark, Luke, or John. As far as we know, he never met Jesus during His earthly ministry. It is not until the book of Acts that Paul comes onto the New Testament scene, and this is several years after Jesus ascended into heaven. When Paul does come into the story, he's very clearly shown to be an enemy of the gospel! So, how could a man who did not know Jesus during His public ministry, and who vehemently opposed Jesus' teaching concerning the kingdom, be God's chosen instrument?

In high school, my sister Kerry decided that she wanted to study medicine. She loved the sciences and even thought about becoming a doctor. She was always a very strong student—more disciplined than I have ever been—so, I'm sure she could've become a doctor if that's what she really wanted to do. During college, though, she realized that medical school might not be in the cards for her. After all, it came with a heavy price tag and demanded many extra years of schooling and a residency. So instead, she investigated pharmacology, medical technology, and a few other related areas of study, but eventually settled on nursing as a career. She continued to do quite well in school, and quickly found a job as a nurse at a local hospital after graduation.

Then an unfortunate thing happened: She discovered she hated nursing. After working as a nurse for a couple of years, she realized that it just wasn't for her. Though she loved studying medicine and helping people, she didn't like many aspects of the actual job. I remember talking with her about it at the time. She told me she thought she'd made a huge mistake. The good thing was that she discovered this early enough to do something about it. Still in her twenties and without any children, Kerry and her husband Jason decided it would be a good idea for her to go back to school, so she could do something she truly enjoyed—something that would be a better fit for her.

After a few more years of schooling, Kerry earned a master's degree in elementary education. It seemed like she was now finally on the right path career-wise, and she began energetically job hunting, looking everywhere for a position as an elementary school teacher. Things were great, except for one important detail: there were no suitable teaching jobs available.

And so, although she was frustrated, Kerry continued her search for a job in her new field for several months. She did eventually find a job teaching, but it wasn't at an elementary school. Instead, someone at Warren G. Harding High School in Bridgeport, Connecticut got their hands on my sister's résumé and decided she would be the perfect candidate for a new teaching position in their medical magnet program. Kerry found herself teaching the medical sciences and offering learning opportunities to a group of disadvantaged high school seniors interested in the field. She could never have done the job without a deep interest in the field of medicine or her nursing background; she would not have been eligible for the position without her master's degree in education. She never could have planned for a more perfect fit. In a role that was part educator, part mentor, and part encourager, Kerry was able to offer a gentle voice of guidance to students in need of direction. The best part was that, instead of just finding a job, Kerry found a ministry and a higher purpose—a calling for a season of her life—and she was extremely blessed for the experience.

Some might call it a happy coincidence that her skill as a nurse and her degree in education made Kerry a good fit for the job at Harding, but I choose to see something different. I choose to see the hand of God at work—redeeming her successes, her failures, and her passions—moving in her life years before she ever could have envisioned herself teaching high school students.

Recently, Kerry sent me a newspaper article about one of her former students, a young woman from very poor and overwhelming circumstances who, through hard work and determination (and, I'm sure, with the prayers of friends and family), graduated from Yale Medical School. Now a doctor, she's returned to Harding High with a foundation she created to mentor and encourage students from urban areas to pursue their dreams. Kerry's investment in the lives of a few high school students is now paying back dividends that never would have occurred had she not made so many "mistakes" while planning her career.

Paul was familiar with a different sort of mistake. Long before he was Paul the apostle, he was Saul of Tarsus, a Pharisee. But Saul was not just any Pharisee; he was poised for greatness. Though originally from Tarsus in Asia Minor, he had grown up in Jerusalem, and was well accustomed with the inner workings of the city's religious hierarchy and culture. He had been fortunate enough to study under the rabbi Gamaliel, a prominent and respected teacher of the Law. Paul was an excellent student, and was looking forward to a prominent position in Jewish society. Paul was also zealous. When he saw the manner in which a new sect, simply called "the Way," was disrupting life in Jerusalem and (in his understanding) twisting the words of God from the Scriptures he had studied so meticulously, he became enraged. He led an effort to crush the movement before it got out of control.

Our first encounter with Paul in the book of Acts is in Chapter 7, during the stoning of a young man named Stephen, a deacon in the church at Jerusalem who had performed miracles and had spoken out boldly concerning Jesus. Saul himself did not cast a stone, though he was complicit in the act by coldly holding the coats of those who did. In that way, he gave approval to the mob scene that was imposing a brand of vigilante justice just outside the city limits of Jerusalem. Following Stephen's death, Paul began to arrest anyone found to be a follower of Jesus. After he had caused many of the Christ-followers living in Jerusalem to scatter, he set his sights on other cities where rumors of the risen Christ had inspired more people to embrace Jesus' teachings and worship Him as Lord, which to Paul was the greatest of blasphemies.

One of the cities where Jesus had gained a following was Damascus. Paul gathered letters from the Jewish authorities in Jerusalem to present to the synagogue officials there, so that if anyone was found following the Way of Jesus, Paul could take them as a prisoner back to Jerusalem to stand trial. It was on the road to Damascus that Paul's life was changed forever by a conversation with Jesus.

Nearing the city, Luke (the writer of Acts) tells us that Paul fell to the ground after being blinded by a powerful light from heaven. Before he could consider what was happening, he heard a voice that said, "Saul, Saul, why do you persecute me?" (Acts 9:4). Paul trembled as he offered a question in response, "Who are you, Lord?" (Acts 9:5). And then, in case he had any doubt about who was speaking to him, the Lord declared, "I am Jesus; it is Me you've been persecuting. Now, get back on your feet.

Continue to the city of Damascus, and there you will be told what you must do for Me."

I would love to have Paul's testimony. It has everything—a dastardly life of sin before meeting Jesus (I mean, trying to destroy the Church is pretty vile), a dramatic vision from heaven that stopped him in his tracks, a divine commission to take the gospel to the far corners of the earth. Paul's story has what it takes to keep people on the edge of their seats in a church service.

My own testimony is slightly more pedestrian. I said the Sinner's Prayer when I was six years old; then again, at least twice a year, between the ages of seven and eleven. When I was twelve, something clicked in Sunday school and I committed my life to Jesus. I think at that point I understood that I was a sinner and that Jesus had died for my sins, so I invited Him to be my Savior. However, it wasn't until I was seventeen that I submitted to Him as Lord, surrendering my life. I had become aware that being a Christian was about more than just avoiding hell, and I had seen Jesus in the lives of teachers and friends who were committed to Him. I decided that I wanted more than just a superficial relationship with Him. Unfortunately for my testimony, I was not snatched from the depths of drug addiction, nor was I rescued from living on the streets. I was not into the Occult or Scientology, and I had never experimented with Ouija boards or been in a gang.

Some people might point to my simple act of faith as a six-year old and identify that as the moment I became a Christian, a child of God. Others would say that the moment didn't come until I understood what it truly meant to need a Savior. Still others would hold the line until I recognized that I needed to make Jesus both Lord *and* Savior of my life. I've met many people with similar stories; they cannot point to one moment in time when they became a Christian. For some, there were many such moments—times of revelation, understanding, and ever-deeper commitments. For others, they honestly can't remember a time when they weren't following Christ. They were brought up in a Christian home and were aware of Jesus from a very young age. While there might have been a moment at the dinner table or just before bed that they invited Him into their lives for the first time, they can't remember when that was.

I don't think it matters whether or not we can remember or can identify a specific moment in our lives when we came to know Christ. The thing that matters is that we do come to know and obey Him. Throughout the centuries, there have been different emphases placed on the conversion experience. Some have made much about being able to rest assured that the issue of eternal security had been settled with the Lord. They would say that if you can't look back on a particular time in your life when you can remember making a commitment to Jesus, you should do it today, just to make sure you have that assurance. Others have noted that what matters is how we live each and every day, so they make it a practice to recommit themselves to the Lord every morning when they wake up. For them, deciding for Christ is not a thing of the past, but of the present and the future. I like the idea of recommitting one's self to Jesus each morning because I think it falls in line with what Jesus said about carrying our crosses daily. Still, I don't think we should get too caught up in semantics, because the important thing is that we're actively following Jesus.

As I said, it was at the age of seventeen—my senior year in high school—that I recognized I needed to submit every area of my life to the Lord. At that time I was deeply concerned with the choices I was making. At that age, there are a lot of important decisions to make, and I wanted to make sure that I didn't make a mistake. After all, I had heard pastors and Christian speakers say dozens of times that God had specific plans for our lives. I didn't want to accidentally screw up those plans by making the wrong choices.

When I got to college, I decided to double-major in biblical & theological studies and economics—just to cover my bases. I wanted to be ready for a life of ministry, but also be prepared to make a good living if God decided that wasn't the life for me. I also decided that I wouldn't date anyone that I wasn't sure I could marry after the first few dates. I realize, to many, that sounds extreme, but I had heard over and over again that God had someone special picked out just for me. Surely He would make it evident after sharing a cup of coffee, a meal in the campus dining hall, and a round of miniature golf if the girl was "the one." I was convinced that the decisions and choices I had made prior to making a firm commitment to the Lord were suspect, because they were made without consulting Jesus. In my mind, it was like I had lost valuable time, so I wanted to do whatever I could to get back on track. It never occurred to me that God could use poor choices, bad judgment, and even sinful mistakes—even those made before I turned to Him in faith— for His good purposes.

In his letter to the Philippian church, Paul gives an account of his old life before everything was changed by his encounter with Jesus on the Damascus road. He writes that he was "circumcised on the eighth day, of the people of Israel, of the tribe of Benjamin, a Hebrew of Hebrews; in regard to the law, a Pharisee; as for zeal, persecuting the church; as for righteousness based on the law, faultless" (Philippians 3:5-6). He recounts this list of accomplishments and personal characteristics—which for him had been a source of pride—only to illustrate the point that anything we think might make us acceptable and pleasing to God is mere refuse. The only thing worth boasting about is Jesus, our Savior and King.

Notice that Paul doesn't say he wasted his life. He doesn't say that studying the law under Gamaliel or being a Jew served no purpose. In fact, he doesn't even say that being a Pharisee in and of itself was a waste. However, immediately after listing the qualifications of his former life that he had once held so dear, he goes on to say, "But whatever were gains to me I now consider loss for the sake of Christ" (Philippians 3:7). In other words, before Paul met Jesus, he had a lot to be proud of, a lot to brag about. In the time and place he lived, he had all the right qualifications to make his way in the world, to think he was something special—special enough to warrant God's favor. But then Jesus came along and changed everything. Paul now considered all of his life's defining characteristics and accomplishments to be nothing at all, that is, compared to his new life with Christ. Any *real* good that Paul was now able to do was only possible because of the Spirit of Jesus working through him.

But what about his old life? Did it have any value for the eternal work to which God had called him or was it wasted time? To put it in twenty-first century terms, *God recycled it*. He took something that was created for one purpose and transformed it for His own eternal purpose. Paul's study of the Hebrew Scriptures, which was originally used to persecute the young church in Jerusalem, would now be used to articulate the mystery of the gospel that God had woven throughout the pages of the Old Testament. Likewise, Paul's legal training and his mastery of logical arguments, which had once provided him with the intellectual firepower to uphold the traditions of his ancestors, would now be used to persuade Jews and Gentiles alike of the truth of the gospel. Even Paul's status as a prominent Jew, once a source of personal pride and self-promotion, now allowed him access to preach the good news of Jesus in synagogues throughout the empire, before crowds of Jews from every walk of life. Likewise, his status a Roman citizen—a rare but valuable commodity for a Jewish man in the first century—gave him opportunities to present the gospel to high ranking Roman officials and to royalty. Paul had planned and worked for a certain type of life—what he thought would be a good life, and even a God-honoring life—but God took that work and used it instead for something far greater than Paul's personal gratification; He used it to change the world.

My wife Melinda and I have a friend who is a bit of a free spirit. Her name is Bridgette and she has a tendency to look at things somewhat differently than most people. When I first met Bridgette at church several years ago, I was struck by the fact that she rarely seemed to care what others thought about her, and she routinely surprised me with things she said and did—not in a bad way, just in a way that kept me guessing, at least until I got to know her better.

A couple of months after I met Bridgette, I was invited to a party she was hosting the Saturday after Thanksgiving. I arrived on time, but I was a few minutes earlier than anyone else, so I helped Bridgette set up for the party—cutting vegetables, mixing punch, moving chairs. While we worked, I asked her if she had done anything exciting over the Thanksgiving weekend. Right on cue, she surprised me. She told me she had spent the previous day at a nearby prison visiting David Berkowitz, the "Son of Sam" killer.

If you're not familiar with the "Son of Sam" murders, allow me to explain why Bridgette's holiday-weekend appointment was such a shock. David Berkowitz was responsible for a series of murders in New York City that took place between July, 1976 and August, 1977. He confessed to killing six people, and is currently serving a life sentence for his crimes. The name "Son of Sam" comes from a letter Berkowitz wrote to the police after one of the shootings, in which he explained that he was being commanded to kill by "father Sam." After he was captured, Berkowitz admitted that "Sam" was a neighbor and that the killings were not ordered by him, but rather by a demon who had possessed Sam's Labrador Retriever.

Bridgette had written to Mr. Berkowitz in prison and had requested permission to visit him after hearing a bit of his story in a church service several Sundays before. You see, David Berkowitz had become a follower of Christ. He met Jesus in prison, and his life was dramatically changed. Bridgette related a bit of his story to me. About ten years into his life sentence, a fellow inmate had shared the gospel with Berkowitz. At first, he rejected the idea that God could love him, but over time, God began to change his heart. He began reading the Bible and he discovered that Jesus had died for him, and that he— David Berkowitz, the "Son of Sam" killer—could be forgiven and receive new life. Bridgette and I were both encouraged by such a drastic specimen of God's grace. She told me how she had seen something in David Berkowitz's eyes: a sense of hope, love, and acceptance—something that was missing in the old photographs taken during the trial and in the early years of his imprisonment. In those days, there was a cold deadness to his eyes; now that cold had been replaced with supernatural warmth.

Today, David Berkowitz joyfully calls himself the "Son of Hope" as he ministers to other prisoners through Bible study, prayer meetings, and personal outreach. He's also had the opportunity to share his testimony with millions of people through television interviews and the Internet, and recently, through the publication of his prison journals (with the proceeds going to the families of his victims). Regardless of the platform, Berkowitz now proclaims the gospel to anyone who will listen. His life is a living testimony, emphatically declaring that no one—no matter how vile or evil their life may be—is beyond hope or outside of God's reach.

God's recycling program is indeed radical. Even David Berkowitz's crimes—as horrible and brutal as they were—are now being used in service to the kingdom. I am not suggesting, in any way, that David Berkowitz's new life in Christ makes his spree of murders any more palpable, nor am I suggesting that the shootings were part of God's plans. The very thought is repulsive. What I am suggesting, however, is that God took something truly evil and used it for something truly good.

The apostle Paul wrote these words: "And we know that in all things God works for the good of those who love him, who have been called according to his purpose" (Romans 8:28). Paul is saying that there is nothing that cannot be redeemed by God and that cannot be used for His good purposes. I wonder if Paul had his own past in mind as he wrote those words. Did he recall how God had used his upbringing and his education—even his zeal for legalistic righteousness—to announce God's grace and mercy? I wonder if he could have imagined a pilgrim like David Berkowitz, and that the "all things" he wrote about included serial murder and the practices of a satanic cult.

As a student and scholar of the Old Testament, Paul would have been thoroughly familiar with the story of Joseph, found in

Genesis, Chapters 37 through 50. Joseph was one of the twelve sons of Jacob—a favorite son, actually. And this special place in his father's heart made his brothers jealous—so jealous that they sold him into slavery in Egypt. There, Joseph encountered more hardships, being falsely accused of attempted rape and thrown into prison. But God used Joseph. He was able to interpret a dream for Pharaoh in which God warned of a coming famine that would decimate the region. As a result, Joseph received special favor from Pharaoh, and was placed in a position of great authority in Egypt, second only to Pharaoh himself. It was from this special position that he enacted a divine plan to save the Egyptian people from the famine that was to come.

Not only did Joseph save the people of Egypt, but he was also able to save his own family—seventy people in all, who would eventually become the Jewish nation. His brothers—the very ones who had years earlier debated whether they should kill him or merely sell him into slavery—now appeared before him to buy grain. Joseph showed mercy to his brothers and forgave them for their terrible crimes, using the opportunity to bless them rather than curse them. There is a touching scene toward the end of the narrative where Joseph reassures his brothers, saying to them, "Don't be afraid. Am I in the place of God? You intended to harm me, but God intended it for good to accomplish what is now being done, the saving of many lives" (Genesis 50:19-20). This is one of my favorite Bible verses because it declares that there is nothing that cannot be redeemed by God—even our own sin can be recycled.

We must, of course, keep in mind that sin has consequences, and I don't want to downplay the seriousness of moral failure. However, that being said, Jesus Christ is bigger than any past failure, mistake, or hardship we may have known or perpetrated. There is nothing so grotesque or malformed that it cannot be redeemed for His own good purposes. The wonder of the gospel is that the ending of the story is even more surprising and beautiful than any of us could ever have imagined.

*"'For I know the plans I have for you,' declares the* LORD, *'plans to prosper you and not to harm you, plans to give you hope and a future.'"* *(Jeremiah 29:11)*

Chapter Eleven: God Recycles
Questions for Reflection & Discussion:

1) What do you think about the author's statement, "There is nothing so grotesque or malformed that it cannot be redeemed for His own good purposes"?

2) Do you find yourself regularly thinking about past regrets or disappointments? If so, ask God to use those things for good. Remember, no matter how ugly or dark something may seem, God can recycle it for His glory. As you reflect, it may help to journal or to share your story with a trusted friend.

3) If you're a Christian, take a few minutes to reflect on your own spiritual journey—your conversion experience (if you can recall it) and your subsequent life in Christ. Do you find yourself growing in your relationship with Jesus? If you are, what do you think has helped you grow? If you're not, why do you think growth isn't occurring?

THE LAST WORD

# Knock, Knock

## Shattered People Need a Physician
## Who Makes House Calls

✢ ✢ ✢

---

# Revelation 3:20
# The Invitation to Conversation

---

✢ ✢ ✢

**SUGGESTED LISTENING**

Rich Mullins: "If I Stand,"
from *Winds of Heaven, Stuff of Earth*
U2: "Yahweh," from *How to Dismantle an Atomic Bomb*

177

# Knock, Knock

## Shattered People Need a Physician Who Makes House Calls

I am convinced the gospel is more powerful than any four-step formula that can be summed up in a tract. I believe the gospel is more real and more personal than anything in creation. When Jesus comes into someone's life, He speaks to their heart and He answers their soul's deepest longings. Jesus *is* the good news. The gospel is indeed a beautiful thing.

As you've seen, this book is a collection of stories—stories about the conversations Jesus had with people who found themselves in a variety of situations, and yes, stories about what Jesus has done in my own life. People from every corner of the earth have carried on conversations with Jesus. The Bible describes this crowd as a "great multitude that no one could count" (Revelation 7:9). These conversations with Jesus continue today, but the dialogues we read about in Scripture are special—they were recorded for our benefit. I think it's fitting that the last such Jesus conversation, found in the book of Revelation, contains these words from Jesus: "Here I am! I stand at the door and knock. If anyone hears my voice and opens the door, I will come in and eat with them, and they with me" (Revelation 3:20). Jesus wants each of us to live in communion with Him. This communion is not a mere ritual, nor is it an impersonal open door. Instead, it's as personal as a meal shared between friends.

In his earthly life, Jesus did many things, but to an outsider, His ministry could be summed up simply by saying that He spent three years walking around. Jesus traveled from town to town, from region to region, and from person to person, speaking the truth in love. Some were met with seemingly harsh words; others were met with mercy. Some were told a parable; others shown a miracle. The aim, however, was always the same—to strip the listener's heart of any callus that might prevent them from knowing Him, and then depending upon, relying upon, surrendering to, and trusting in Him.

My hope is that you might have seen yourself in at least one of these stories. Maybe it was in Jesus' encounter with the rich, confident, young ruler; maybe in His talk with the woman at the well, hiding in the darkness. Maybe you identified with Pilate, tucking truth away because it's inconvenient and might exact a price too costly to endure. Perhaps you often feel like Nicodemus, only willing to come to Jesus in secret. If you're like me, your story is a mixture of some pain, some joy, some shame, and a lot of wandering. There are no easy answers to most of the struggles we deal with, but Jesus offers each of us a new life. This new life will not erase the challenges you might be facing, and it may not make your everyday life easier, but this new life is a life of promise... a promise of hope and joy—in the life to come, true, but in *this* life—here and now, as well. It's a life where faith is the only requirement necessary to receive forgiveness and a fresh start. It's a life where the King of the Universe will sit down and have lunch with you.

I love that we're having this conversation via the pages of a book. There can be no high-pressure sales pitch, and no putting you on the spot (I wouldn't want to do that anyway). You can read this at your own pace, and take as much time as you need to think about the content of these pages. However, I hope that sometime soon—perhaps today, perhaps in the next few days—you'll find a comfortable place at home or in a secluded location, some place where you can be alone.[40] I hope that you'll take some time to meet with Jesus.

If you've never entered into conversation with Him before, don't worry; there are no special or magic words required. Just be honest with Him. Share with Him whatever is weighing on your heart—your fears, your doubts, your shame—anything that could get in the way of opening yourself up to God's love. If you don't think you're ready to open yourself up entirely, that's okay too. Just share with Him what you're ready to share; He'll meet you where you are. I believe that in time, as you grow more comfortable, you'll find that it's easier to share your burdens with Jesus.

Remember that, as in any good relationship, you must listen as well as talk. And how will Jesus speak to you? My guess is that it will probably not be with an audible voice. However, I do believe that Jesus does speak to our hearts in a way that is much deeper and more indelible than mere words could ever be. But we need to be still and listen. You may also find that He speaks to you through the pages of Scripture, or through other people who know and love the Lord. Whatever the means, Jesus promises to be with you, if you have invited Him into your life.

---

40 I find that I am often better able to open up to and hear from Jesus outside—somewhere away from many of the distractions of modern life. But that's just me. I know some who have a favorite spot at home—a comfortable chair or a seat by a window—where they meet with God. The important thing is that you're at ease, and that you can focus on Him.

If you already know Jesus, I would still invite you to set aside some time to meet with Him. As I shared earlier in the book, knowing Jesus is not a one-time event; it's rather more like a journey. As you spend time with Him and invite Him into those areas of your life that may have previously been reserved for you alone, you'll find that your relationship grows, and that the journey becomes sweeter and more exciting. I have the privilege of knowing a few people in their seventies and eighties who have been walking with Jesus for more than fifty years. What each of them would tell you is that knowing Jesus never gets old, and that their journey with Him has been, and still is, the greatest adventure of their lives. My hope is that you will find this to be true in your own life.

✡ ✡ ✡

*"I no longer call you servants, because servants do not know their master's business. Instead, I have called you friends, for everything that I learned from my Father I have made known to you." (John 15:15)*

# Acknowledgements

I'd like to express my gratitude to good friends who read early incarnations of this book: Don Hay, Julie Davis, Rebecca Henry, Janell Huenemeier, and Bridgette Veale. Thank you for your honest feedback, your thoughtful critiques, and your encouragement to keep going. But most of all, thank you for laughing at the parts that were supposed to be funny.

Thank you to my sister Kerry for having my back (even when it's probably not necessary) and for letting it slide that an early version of this manuscript left you out of the story. Special thanks to the Huenemeiers, Carons, Cockrums, Holmeses, McKays, Grecos, Austins, and to "Red hot" Ruby for not assuming I was joking when I announced I was going to write a book. Thanks for the love.

I owe a bit of gratitude to Joe Gattuso, my editor and publisher, for seeing something worth digging up and polishing in the sample chapters I initially sent to The Wild Olive Press. Thanks for your patience during the editing process and for believing this book is something that should be read by people outside of my immediate family.

Also, special thanks go to Kevin Butterfield for writing the foreword. I am honored to have you be a part of this project.

Your family is officially my favorite in the Southern Hemisphere.

Thank you to Mary Precup, who first gave me the opportunity to write and get paid for it. I hope that as you read this book, you'll resist the urge to pull out your green pen (though I know that brings you joy).

I am also grateful to the faculty and staff at Christian Heritage School for faithfully modeling the Christian life for so many years, and for teaching the Bible to kids who don't always want to hear it.

I'd like to convey heartfelt thanks to Johannes Gutenburg for inventing movable type. This project would not have been possible without your innovative spirit and I don't think you get thanked enough. Well done, sir.

A note of thanks is also due to the fine people at the American Broadcasting Company and to the producers of *LOST*. Without the lengthy hiatus that stretches from May to January, I wouldn't have been able to focus long enough to finish this book. Your show makes my head hurt, but thank you all the same.

And, of course, thank you to Melinda for reading every paragraph as they were written, and for believing that I can do anything (that doesn't require being able to clap to a beat or sing in tune, of course).

# About the Author

John Greco lives in Connecticut with his wife Melinda, where they drive around in a van solving mysteries. Okay, their "van" is actually a Subaru, and they haven't yet solved a mystery. However, if a mystery presented itself, they would certainly give it their best shot. John is finishing up the final course requirements for a Master of Divinity degree at Gordon-Conwell Theological Seminary. After graduation, he hopes to be engaged in full-time pastoral ministry. When he's not poring over Greek, Hebrew, church history, or theology, he goes to work at a place that's kind of like the British version of the television show *The Office*, only no one speaks with a British accent and it's not as funny. His articles about faith and life have appeared on relevantmagazine.com, at the Burnside Writers Collective, and in several other print and online publications. John is a bit uncomfortable writing in the third person like this. This is his first book.

Made in the USA
Lexington, KY
04 March 2010